Popular French Cookbook

Popular French Cookbook

Mary Berry

LONGMEADOW
PRESS

Contents

Photographs on frontispiece and pages 7, 11, 19, 43, 51, 55, 59, 94 by courtesy of Syndication International
Photographs on pages 15, 23, 27, 35, 63, 67, 71, 83, 87 by courtesy of Paf International

Frontispiece: Pâté Maison

This edition first published in the USA by
Longmeadow Press,
PO Box 16, Rowayton Station,
Norwalk, Connecticut 06353

© 1972, 1977 Octopus Books Limited

ISBN 0 7064 0627 3

Produced by Mandarin Publishers Limited,
Hong Kong
Printed in Hong Kong

WEIGHTS AND MEASURES

All measurements in this book are based on Imperial weights and measures, with American equivalents given in parenthesis

Measurements in *weight* in the Imperial and American system are the same.

Measurements in *volume* are different, and the following table shows the equivalents:

Spoon measurements

Imperial	U.S.
1 teaspoon (5 ml.)	$1\frac{1}{4}$ teaspoons
1 tablespoon (20 ml.)	$1\frac{1}{4}$ tablespoons (abbrev: T)

Level spoon measurements are used in all the recipes

Liquid measurements

1 Imperial pint	20 fluid ounces
1 American pint	16 fluid ounces
1 American cup	8 fluid ounces

Introduction

There is a tendency to confuse French cooking with *elaborate* cooking. Many a sound cook has shrunk from tackling French dishes for fear that as the recipe progresses from one complicated step to the next she will lose her way and the final result will be a disaster.

Yet nothing could be further from the truth. Certainly there *are* elaborate French dishes but these are mainly confined to professional chefs and great restaurants. The French housewife has no more time to spend in the kitchen than her equivalent in other countries. Meals in a French household, therefore, tend to be simple. But simple certainly does not mean dull. Basic dishes gain a subtlety of flavour from the addition of wine, herbs or garlic, sometimes all three. French cooks understand that appetites are best stimulated by appealing to three senses – sight and smell as well as taste, so that care is taken with presentation as well as with cooking.

It has been said that the French think more of their stomachs than of anything else, that they hold eating in far higher esteem than, for example, making love or making money. You don't have to spend much time in France before coming to the same conclusion. The midday meal is the highspot of the French day. Not for them an hour's lunchtime or doughy sandwich, hastily bought and absentmindedly devoured. Most Frenchmen make a bee-line for home when the morning's work is over, home to a wonderfully aromatic smell which greets them as they enter the front door, home to a colourfully laid table and a bottle of *vin ordinaire* usually drunk from tumblers. French cooking is not necessarily expensive. More often than not, it is the reverse. The French, by and large, are incredibly frugal. What one housewife would throw away, a Frenchwoman would probably regard as the basis of the next meal. Bones go into a stockpot (why spend money on bouillon cubes?) stale bread may be crisped in the oven, or over-dried and turned into breadcrumbs, or served in soup as crôutons. Bacon rind may be fried and used as garnish, bacon fat rendered down and used in cooking. Left-over potato makes a thickening for soup.

The characteristic French knack of making something out of nothing enables the French to eat well. Add to this, their superb understanding of what makes a dish, what particular ingredient in a recipe – and how much – will turn a mundane meal into a creation, and there is little wonder that French cooking is admired and imitated throughout the world.

A study of French cooking shows how much reliance is put on certain ingredients, namely wine, garlic, herbs, mushrooms, oil and vinegar. Because they do play so important a part, I will deal with them here under separate headings.

PISSALADIÈRE

Wine

The importance of wine in cookery lies in the flavour it gives the finished dish. Some people are afraid to use wine for fear that it will make the dish alcoholic. In fact, whether the cooking is long and slow, as in a casserole, or rapid, as when the wine is added to a quickly-cooked dish and reduced by fast boiling to a sauce, the alcohol content is burnt out. What remains is the essence of the wine, delicate, appetizing and unmistakable.

The wine to use can be as cheap or as expensive as you like. You may think that the quality does not matter since it is being cooked, but a better wine adds a richness of flavour that is far superior to that of its cheaper equivalent. Sometimes, it is worth while sneaking a glassful of the wine that is to be served at the table. In this case, the bottle, if a white wine, can be recorked and chilled in the refrigerator; if red, it should be left uncorked to reach room temperature.

Unless the wine is to be drunk later, it is better to buy a half bottle than a whole one. Unused wine may be corked up in a small bottle and stored in a refrigerator, but do not keep it longer than two or three days. Sour wine will certainly not improve a dish. White wine, on the whole, keeps better than red.

Some recipes call for fortified wines, such as Marsala, Madeira or sherry. These fortified wines, unlike ordinary ones, need not be cooked. A spoonful of sherry, for example, may be added to consommé with excellent effect.

Sometimes, spirits are used to flambé a dish. In this case the brandy, or whatever spirit is chosen, is first warmed in a soup ladle to ensure that it will flame, then set alight and the burning liquid poured over the meat or pancakes in the pan. The pan should be shaken gently to spread the flames. When they die down, the alcohol will have burnt away and taken with it any excess grease.

Sweet dishes may be enhanced by adding liqueur to them. If this sounds expensive, consider buying a miniature bottle, which will not add a great deal to the cost of the meal but will add enormously to its quality.

Garlic

Garlic and the Continent seem synonymous to many people. Appreciation of the culinary virtues of garlic has remained the prerogative of the Continent.

The essence of using garlic in cooking is restraint. Its flavour must never be allowed to dominate the dish – far better to use too little than too much. In salads, for example, just rubbing round the salad bowl with a clove of garlic will give the salad a subtle lift. A little garlic in butter on French bread makes a dish in itself.

Fresh garlic is always better than any form of dried garlic, and the best way of using it is to squeeze it through a garlic press. The use of a press prevents the very persistent smell of garlic from lingering on the chopping board or on your hands. And, incidentally, the press has other uses in the kitchen. It is excellent for extracting the juice from onions or fresh herbs.

Herbs

Herbs, of course, are used in most forms of cooking, but often rather conservatively. The French, however, call on a wide range of herbs and use them in a great variety of ways. Country families in France grow them in their rather formal gardens, gather them and dry them in bunches suspended from the kitchen ceiling. The bunches of drying herbs make an attractive addition to kitchen décor and have the added advantage that they are always on hand. The modern commercial process of drying herbs is so quick that the herbs retain most of their colour and flavour, and the dried herbs we buy now are vastly superior to those of the past.

The French make an excellent herb dressing for salads by steeping herbs in the dressing in a bottle for about five days. At the end of that time the dressing is strained and rebottled. The herbs have gone, but their delicate aroma remains.

Mushrooms

Mushrooms figure in so many French recipes that they are worth a study in themselves. In a French market there may be as many as eight different varieties of mushroom on sale, each with its own subtle flavour. The mushroom of the woodlands tastes quite different from the mushroom of the fields, and the French, with typical thoroughness, are well aware of the difference such variety makes to the final dish. I feel, however, that it is wiser to leave experimentation to the experts on edible fungi. Where mushrooms have been used in the recipes in this book, I have kept to the ordinary kind, known all over the world.

Oil

Two different kinds of oil are commonly used in France. Olive oil is used mainly for mayonnaise and dressings, groundnut oil, which is much cheaper, for frying. A good olive oil does not have a strong flavour. Groundnut oil (*huile d'arachides*) is almost flavourless, and some people prefer it for salads, using herbs, seasoning, vinegar and lemon juice to sharpen the taste of the dressing or mayonnaise.

Vinegar

A malt vinegar salesman would have a thin time in France, except possibly from young French girls who rinse their hair in malt vinegar. In French cookery, vinegar is almost always distilled from white or red wine. Tarragon vinegar is wine vinegar flavoured with tarragon and for some dishes it is preferred to straight wine vinegar.

Cider vinegar may sometimes be substituted for the more expensive wine vinegar.

Tips for kitchen users

By and large, the French are not gadget-minded and seem content to go on using the equipment with which their grandmothers were happy. Really sharp knives are undoubtedly top of the list. For some reason, the French are quite expert at making really good, stainless steel kitchen knives. Even the cheap ones, found in any inexpensive department store in France, need no more than normal care to keep a good edge on them.

The French are also keen on graters, of varying sizes, each with a number of different blades, with which they can slice, shred or purée. Useful ideas worth copying from a French kitchen are: making French dressing in quantity, which may be bottled and stored in a cold place; making mayonnaise in quantity and storing the surplus in the refrigerator; keeping a vanilla pod in a jar of sugar, (the vanilla-flavoured sugar thus produced is useful for making custards, etc.); keeping seasonings in a box near the cooker, handy for adjusting the seasoning of a dish during the cooking.

Finally, if you are shopping in France or ordering from a French menu, don't forget that the French for chicory is *endive* and the French for endive is *chicorie*.

FRENCH ONION SOUP

CURTAIN RAISERS: BEGINNINGS

In France, these are known generally as *hors d'oeuvres*, but this term, outside France, has a specific meaning. Better, I think, to call the first course beginnings, for this is what it is – the beginning of a meal which should leave both you and your guests mellow and satisfied. The course should have two virtues – first, it should titillate the palate but not destroy the appetite, and, second, it should be easy to prepare and to serve, so that you, as cook, may concentrate on the main course without worry. Most of the recipes that follow may be prepared beforehand.

French Onion Soup

Soupe à l'oignon

$\frac{1}{2}$ lb. onions, sliced
1 oz. (2T) butter
1 teaspoon castor (superfine) sugar
1 tablespoon (1$\frac{1}{4}$T) flour
1$\frac{1}{2}$ pints (3$\frac{3}{4}$ cups) beef stock

salt
pepper
4 slices French bread
2 oz. ($\frac{1}{2}$ cup) grated Gruyère cheese

Brown the onions slowly in the butter. Add the sugar and cook for a few minutes. Add the flour and cook for 1 minute. Add the stock and bring to the boil, stirring. Simmer 20 minutes then add salt and pepper if necessary.
Toast one side of the bread then sprinkle cheese on the untoasted side. Grill until the cheese has melted. Put a slice of bread in each soup bowl and pour the soup on top.
Serves 4

Mushroom Cream Soup

Potage crème de champignons

2 tablespoons (2½T) cooking
  oil
1 oz. (2T) butter
2 onions, finely chopped
¼ lb. (1¼ cups) mushrooms,
  finely chopped
3 tablespoons (3¾T) flour
1¼ pints (3 cups) beef stock

¼ pint thin (coffee) cream
salt
pepper
pinch of grated nutmeg
little thick (heavy) cream
1 tablespoon (1¼T) chopped
  parsley

Heat the oil in a pan, then add the butter. Add the onions and
cook until tender, then add the mushrooms and cook for 3
minutes.
Blend in the flour and cook for 1 minute. Gradually add the
stock, stirring. Bring to the boil then simmer for about 5
minutes until thick and smooth.
Add the thin cream, seasoning and nutmeg and simmer for 3
minutes. Finally stir in the thick cream and parsley.
Serves 4

Smoked Mackerel Paté

Pâté de maquereaux fumés
*Smoked mackerel can be bought at a large fishmongers or delicatessen. The
pâté keeps well in a home freezer.*

2 smoked mackerel, skinned
  and boned
3 oz. cream cheese spread
juice of ½ lemon

10 oz. (1¼ cups) butter, melted
salt
pepper

Purée the mackerel in a blender, or mash well with a fork.
Gradually add the remaining ingredients and blend until
smooth, or mash the mackerel with the cream cheese and then
add the other ingredients.
Turn into small ramekins and chill before serving.
Serves 6

Cauliflower Soup

Soupe au choufleur

2 oz. ($\frac{1}{4}$ cup) butter
1 large onion, sliced
1 garlic clove, crushed
1 medium cauliflower, in
    sprigs
1$\frac{3}{4}$ pints (4$\frac{1}{2}$ cups) chicken
    stock
salt

pepper
4 tablespoons (5T) thin
    (coffee) cream

Garnish:
2 slices toast
1 tablespoon (1$\frac{1}{4}$T) chopped
    parsley

Heat the butter in a large, heavy pan. Add the onion and garlic and fry slowly until soft. Add the cauliflower, water and stock cubes then cover and simmer for 1 hour.
Sieve the soup or purée in a blender. Return it to the pan and check seasoning. Stir in the cream and re-heat the soup almost to simmering point.
Cut the bread in $\frac{1}{2}$-inch cubes and scatter on top of the soup with the parsley just before serving.
Serves 6

Garlic Bread

Pain à l'ail

1 French loaf
2 oz. ($\frac{1}{4}$ cup) butter
1 garlic clove, crushed

1 tablespoon (1$\frac{1}{4}$T) chopped
    parsley

Cut the loaf in 1-inch slices, almost through to the bottom crust. Blend together the remaining ingredients. Spread the mixture between the slices of bread.
Wrap the loaf in foil and cook at 425°F, Gas Mark 7 for 15-20 minutes. Serve hot, divided in slices.
Serves 6

Fresh Herb Paté

Pâté aux fines herbes
Make this the day before it is needed so that the flavours blend well.

6 oz. ($\frac{3}{4}$ cup) rich cream
    cheese
$\frac{1}{4}$ pint ($\frac{1}{2}$ cup + 2T) thick
    (heavy) cream, lightly
    whipped
$\frac{1}{2}$ teaspoon freshly chopped
    thyme

$\frac{1}{2}$ teaspoon freshly chopped
    dill
1 teaspoon freshly chopped
    chives
salt
pepper

Blend together the cheese and cream. Stir in the herbs and
seasoning. Turn into a $\frac{3}{4}$ pint (2 cups) dish and chill before
serving. Serve with crisp biscuits.
Serves 4 as a starter

Brandade of Kipper

Brandade de harengs fumés
A smooth smoked fish pâté

2 large kippers
1$\frac{1}{2}$ oz. (3T) butter
2 teaspoons lemon juice
5 tablespoons (6$\frac{1}{4}$T) thin
    (coffee) cream

5 tablespoons (6$\frac{1}{4}$T) thick
    (heavy) cream, lightly
    whipped
salt
pepper

Dot the kippers with butter and grill (broil) for 10 minutes.
Reserve any butter and juices and skin and bone the fish.
Purée the kippers in a blender with the juices, or mash with a
fork until smooth. When the paste is cold, stir in lemon juice
and single cream. Mix until smooth then fold in the double
cream. Check the seasoning, turn into 6 individual ramekins
and chill until 1 hour before the meal. Serve with hot toast
and butter.
Serves 6

Mussels Marinière

Moules à la marinière
When buying mussels, allow 1½ pints (4 cups) per person. Take care not to overcook them. They only take a few minutes, just until the shells are open.

6 pints (15 cups) fresh
   mussels
1 oz. (2T) butter
4 small onions, chopped
4 parsley stalks
2 sprigs fresh thyme or
   ¼ teaspoon dried thyme
1 bay leaf
freshly ground black
   pepper

½ pint (1¼ cups) dry white
   wine
salt
chopped parsley

Beurre Manié:
1 oz. (2T) butter, blended
   with 1 tablespoon (1¼T)
   flour

Scrape and clean each mussel with a strong knife, removing every trace of seaweed, mud and beard. Wash very well and discard any mussels which do not close tightly.
Melt the butter in a large pan, add the onions and fry until soft but not coloured. Add the herbs, pepper and wine and then the mussels. Cover with a tightly fitting lid and cook quickly, shaking the pan constantly, until the mussels open – about 5 to 6 minutes. Lift the mussels out of the pan, discard the empty half of each shell and keep the rest hot in a covered serving dish.
Reduce the cooking liquor to about ½ pint (1¼ cups). Remove the fresh thyme, parsley stalks and bay leaf. Drop the butter and flour mixture into the simmering stock a teaspoon at a time and whisk until the stock is smooth and thickened. Check seasoning.
Pour the sauce over the mussels and scatter with plenty of chopped parsley. Serve with French bread and butter or garlic bread, see page 14.
Finger bowls are a help as picking up mussels is a messy process. You also need a dish for the empty shells.
Serves 4

Bouillabaisse

3 lb. fish to include:
mackerel
plaice (flounder)
whiting
rock salmon (rockfish)
1 cooked crab (optional)
1 small, split lobster tail or
   crawfish tail
$\frac{1}{2}$ pint (1 cup) cooked prawns
   (shrimp)
few cooked mussels
4 tablespoons (5T) olive oil

2 onions, chopped
1 leek, sliced
2 pints (5 cups) fish liquor
4 tomatoes, skinned,
   de-seeded and chopped
$\frac{1}{4}$ teaspoon dried fennel
$\frac{1}{8}$ teaspoon powdered saffron
1 bay leaf
3 sprigs parsley
salt, pepper
6-8 slices French bread

Ask the fishmonger to fillet and skin the mackerel, plaice, whiting and rock salmon but keep the skin and bones for stock. Prepare the crab, if used, and the lobster or crawfish tail. Shell the prawns but keep the mussels in their shells. Put the skin, bones and shells from the fish and shellfish in a pan with $2\frac{1}{2}$ pints (6 cups) water. Bring to the boil and simmer for 20 minutes, then strain off the fish liquor.
Heat the oil in a large pan, add the onion and leek and fry slowly until soft but not coloured. Add the mackerel and plaice, cut in chunks, to the pan and cook gently for 10 minutes, then add the remaining fish, in chunks, fish liquor and all other ingredients except the French bread. Simmer for about 10 minutes until the fish is cooked.
Check the seasoning, discard the bay leaf and parsley. Put the bread in a tureen and pour in the fish mixture.
Serves 6-8

Eggs in Consommé

Oeufs en gelée

15 oz. can consommé
4 teaspoons powdered
  gelatine

6 small eggs
4 oz. pâté de foie truffé

Put the consommé and gelatine in a pan, leave for 2 minutes
then heat gently, without boiling, until the gelatine has
dissolved. Cool the mixture.
Soft boil the eggs for 6 minutes then remove the shells
carefully and put the eggs in cold water.
Pour $\frac{1}{4}$-inch of consommé into six individual ramekin dishes
and leave in a cold place to set. Put an egg in each ramekin
and pour over sufficient consommé just to cover. Leave again
until set. Spread a layer of pâté on top of each ramekin and
leave in a cold place until needed.
Just before serving, turn them out and serve with warm
French bread.
Serves 6

Pâté Maison

$\frac{3}{4}$ lb. smoked bacon joint,
  boned and rolled
1 tablespoon ($1\frac{1}{4}$T) clear
  honey
2 teaspoons soft brown sugar
8 cloves
6 peppercorns
$\frac{1}{8}$ teaspoon dried thyme
1 small bay leaf
$\frac{1}{2}$ lb. pigs' liver
1 slice brown bread, with
  crusts removed
$\frac{1}{4}$ lb. pork sausage meat

2 oz. ($\frac{1}{4}$ cup) lard, melted
1 small garlic clove, crushed
grated rind of $\frac{1}{2}$ lemon
1 onion, chopped
$\frac{1}{8}$ teaspoon ground allspice
$\frac{1}{8}$ teaspoon ground nutmeg
$\frac{1}{2}$ teaspoon salt
$\frac{1}{8}$ teaspoon pepper
1 egg
1-2 tablespoons ($1\frac{1}{4}$-$2\frac{1}{2}$T) dry
  sherry
1 large lemon or 5 rashers of
  bacon

Put the bacon in a pan with the honey, sugar, cloves, peppercorns, herbs and sufficient water just to cover. Cover with a lid, bring to boiling point and simmer for 35 minutes then remove the bacon from the pan and take off the rind. Mince the bacon, liver and bread finely then blend with all the other ingredients except the whole lemon.

Slice the lemon very thinly and use to line the base and sides of a greased 2 pint (5 cup) round or oval ovenproof casserole (if preferred, line with rashers of bacon). Fill with the pâté, cover with a lid, or foil, and place in a meat tin, half filled with hot water. Cook at 325°F, Gas Mark 3 for 2 hours. Allow to cool completely before serving.

Serves 6

Eggs Mornay

Oeufs à la mornay

4 eggs
1 oz. (2T) butter
1 oz. (4T) flour
$\frac{1}{4}$ pint (1$\frac{1}{4}$ cups) milk
2 oz. ($\frac{1}{2}$ cup) Gruyère cheese, grated

1 oz. ($\frac{1}{4}$ cup) Parmesan cheese, grated
$\frac{1}{2}$ teaspoon made mustard
salt
pepper

Boil the eggs for only 8 minutes so they are not completely hard. Cool under running cold water. Remove the shells carefully.

Melt the butter in a pan, add the flour and cook for 1 minute. Stir in the milk and bring to boiling point, stirring constantly. Simmer for 2 minutes, remove the pan from the heat and stir in most of the cheese. Add mustard and plenty of seasoning. Cut the eggs in half lengthways. Arrange in an ovenproof serving dish. Spoon over the sauce. Sprinkle with the remaining cheese. Brown under the grill (broiler). Serve with a green salad and toast.

Serves 4

Mushroom Vols Au Vent

Vol-au-vent de champignons

6 oz. puff pastry, made with
   6 oz. (1½ cups) flour, 6 oz.
   (¾ cup) butter

or

11 oz. packet frozen puff pastry
1 egg blended with 1
   tablespoon (1¼T) water

Filling:
1½ oz. (3T) butter
6 oz. (2 cups) mushrooms,
   sliced
1 oz. (4T) flour
½ pint (1¼ cups) milk
salt
pepper

Roll the pastry out ¼ inch thick, on a well floured board. Cut six 3 inch circles with a pastry cutter. Make a smaller cut ¼ inch inside each case but do not cut completely through the pastry. Place on an ungreased baking tray and chill in the refrigerator for 30 minutes.

Brush the tops of the cases with egg glaze and bake at 400°F, Gas Mark 6 for 20 minutes, or until well risen and golden brown. Remove from the baking sheet and cool on a wire rack. Carefully remove the 'lids' with a sharp knife and scoop out any uncooked mixture.

Melt the butter for the filling in a pan. Add the mushrooms, cover and cook for 2 minutes. Blend in the flour and cook for 1 minute. Blend in the milk and bring to the boil then simmer for 2 minutes. Season well with salt and pepper.

Fill the prepared cases with the mixture and replace the lids. Re-heat at 400°F, Gas Mark 6 for 10-15 minutes.

Serves 6 as a starter

Pissaladière

Rich shortcrust pastry:
5 oz. (1¼ cups) plain flour
½ teaspoon salt
2½ oz. (5T) butter
1 egg
Filling:
1 tablespoon (1¼T) olive oil
1 oz. (2T) butter
1½ lb. onions, finely sliced

½ teaspoon salt
⅛ teaspoon pepper
⅛ teaspoon ground nutmeg
3 egg yolks
3 tablespoons (3¾T) milk
¼ lb. (½ cup) cream cheese
Garnish:
about 16 anchovy fillets
16 black olives

Make the pastry in the usual way, adding sufficient egg to
bind the mixture together. Wrap it in foil and chill for 2
hours. Heat the oil in a pan, add the butter and cook the
onions, slowly, covered, for 30 minutes until soft and pale
golden, then add seasoning and nutmeg and put on one side.
Use the pastry to line a shallow 9-inch fluted flan tin placed on
a baking tray. Line with greaseproof paper and baking beans,
or foil, and bake 'blind' at 400°F, Gas Mark 6 for 20 minutes.
Remove the beans and paper, or foil.
Blend together the egg yolks, milk and cheese, then mix with
the onion. Pour the filling into the pastry case and cook at
350°F, Gas Mark 4 for 20 minutes or until just set. Arrange the
anchovy fillets in a lattice on top of the filling with the black
olives, then cook for a further 10 minutes.
Serves 6

Stuffed Peppers

Poivrons farcis

4 large green peppers

Filling:
1 small aubergine (egg plant)
3 tablespoons (3¾T) olive oil
1 large onion, chopped
1 oz. (4T) flour

12 oz. cooked ham, cubed
pepper
½ teaspoon dried oregano
½ pint (1¼ cups) chicken stock
2 tablespoons (2½T) tomato
  purée
salt

24

Cut the peppers in half lengthways, remove the seeds and stem. Cut the aubergine (egg plant) in $\frac{1}{4}$ inch dice.

Heat the oil in a pan, add the aubergine (egg plant) and onion. Cover and fry gently until soft, for about 5 minutes. Stir in the flour, then add the remaining ingredients for the filling and bring to boiling point.

Put the halved peppers in a shallow ovenproof dish. Fill with the mixture and cover with foil. Bake at 350°F, Gas Mark 4 for about 10 minutes or until the peppers are soft.

Serves 4

Cheese Soufflé

Soufflé au fromage

If you are making this soufflé for guests, get it to the white sauce stage then add the yolks and cheese. Fifty minutes or so before serving whisk the egg whites until stiff and fold into the mixture. Turn into the prepared soufflé dish and cook as below

3 oz. (6T) butter
2 oz. ($\frac{1}{2}$ cup) plain (all-purpose) flour
$\frac{1}{2}$ pint (1$\frac{1}{4}$ cups) milk
1 oz. ($\frac{1}{4}$ cup) grated Parmesan cheese

3 oz. ($\frac{3}{4}$ cup) Gruyère cheese, grated
salt
pepper
1 teaspoon Dijon mustard
3 large eggs, separated

Butter a 2 pint (5 cup) soufflé dish. Melt the butter in a pan. Stir in the flour, then blend in the milk. Bring to the boil, stirring constantly, then simmer for 3 minutes. Remove the pan from the heat and beat in the cheese, seasoning and mustard. Beat in the egg yolks, one at a time.

Whisk the egg whites until stiff, then fold into the cheese mixture. Turn into the prepared dish and cook at 375°F, Gas Mark 5 for about 45 minutes, until the soufflé is well risen and the top is set and slightly crusty. Serve at once.

Serves 4

Individual Quiches

Petites quiches
These small tarts make a substantial beginning to a summer dinner party.

Pastry:
6 oz. shortcrust pastry made
   with 6 oz. (1½ cups) flour,
   etc., see recipe below

Filling:
4 oz. shelled shrimps or
   prawns

1 egg
4 oz. carton (½ cup) thin
   (coffee) cream
1 oz. (¼ cup) Cheddar cheese,
   finely grated
¼ teaspoon salt
⅛ teaspoon pepper

Use the pastry to line 12 individual patty tins. Bake 'blind' at
400°F, Gas Mark 6 for 7 minutes. Remove the paper and
baking beans, or foil.
Divide the shrimps or prawns between the pastry cases. Blend
together the remaining ingredients and spoon into the cases.
Bake at 350°F, Gas Mark 4 for about 20 minutes or until the
filling is pale golden and lightly set.
Serves 6 as a starter

Shortcrust Pastry

Pâte brisée

8 oz. (2 cups) plain (all-
   purpose) flour
½ teaspoon salt

2 oz. (¼ cup) butter
2 oz. (¼ cup) lard
about 8 teaspoons cold water

Sift the flour and salt into a bowl. Cut the fats in small pieces
then rub into the flour with the tips of the fingers until the
mixture resembles fine breadcrumbs. Add enough water to
mix to a firm dough. Roll out thinly on a floured board and
use as required.

Those with modest appetites may willingly forgo the third course. They may even dispense with the first. But the main course is always the star turn. The art of French cookery is typified in the following recipes, which make full use of wine, herbs and garlic.

Beef Fillet in Pastry

Filet de boeuf en croûte
When entertaining, the prepared dish can be left in the refrigerator for up to 12 hours before cooking.

2 oz. ($\frac{1}{4}$ cup) butter
$1\frac{1}{2}$ lb. fillet of beef
1 garlic clove, crushed
$\frac{1}{4}$ lb. ($1\frac{1}{3}$ cups) mushrooms, sliced
4 tablespoons (5T) Madeira wine

$\frac{1}{2}$ teaspoon salt
$\frac{1}{8}$ teaspoon pepper
4 oz. puff pastry, made with 4 oz. (1 cup) flour, etc. or $7\frac{1}{2}$ oz. frozen puff pastry
milk for glazing

Melt the butter in a pan, add the beef and garlic and fry quickly for 15 minutes (or 10 minutes for a rare centre to the beef, 25 minutes for a well-done fillet), turning on all sides. Remove the beef from the pan, add the mushrooms and cook until soft. Put the Madeira in the pan and simmer until the liquid has reduced by half. Remove the pan from the heat and add seasoning.
Roll out the pastry to a rectangle, about 9 by 12 inches. This will vary according to the size of the fillet. Put the beef in the centre of the pastry with the mushrooms on top and spoon over the sauce. Fold over the pastry, moisten the edges and seal firmly with the fold on top so that juices do not run out. Chill for 30 minutes.
Place on a baking tray, glaze with milk and cook at 400°F, Gas Mark 6 for about 25 minutes until the pastry is golden. Serve with Madeira Sauce, see page 32.
Serves 4-6

Burgundy Beef

Boeuf bourguignonne

$1\frac{1}{2}$ lb. chuck steak
1 oz. (2T) bacon fat
6 oz. unsmoked streaky
   bacon, rinded and cut in
   $\frac{1}{2}$ inch wide strips
$\frac{1}{2}$ oz. (2T) flour
$\frac{1}{2}$ pint beef stock
$\frac{1}{4}$ pint red wine
1 bay leaf

$\frac{1}{2}$ level teaspoon dried mixed
   herbs
sprig of parsley
about $\frac{1}{2}$ level teaspoon salt
$\frac{1}{8}$ level teaspoon pepper
$\frac{1}{4}$ lb. small, even-sized onions,
   peeled
2 oz. button mushrooms

Cut the steak into $1\frac{1}{2}$ inch squares. Melt the bacon fat in a fairly large pan and fry the bacon for a few minutes until it begins to turn brown. Lift the bacon out of the pan and into a 3-pint (8-cup) casserole and then fry the steak in fat remaining in the pan until it is brown all over.

Add the steak to the bacon in the casserole and pour off all but 2 tablespoons ($2\frac{1}{2}$T) of the fat. Blend the flour with the fat and continue to cook until it has browned. Remove the pan from the heat and stir in stock and wine. Return the pan to the heat and bring the liquor to boiling point. Simmer until it has thickened.

Add the bay leaf, herbs, parsley and seasoning, adding only a little of the salt, as the bacon may be salty. Pour the liquor over the meat, cover the casserole and simmer gently in the oven at 325°F, Gas Mark 3 for $1\frac{1}{2}$ hours.

Add the onions and mushrooms to the casserole and cook it for a further hour or until the meat is really tender. Check seasoning and add more salt and pepper if necessary. Skim off any fat on the surface.

Serves 6

Pot Roast

Boeuf à la mode
There is no need to use prime beef for this recipe.

$\frac{1}{2}$ pint (1$\frac{1}{4}$ cups) beef stock
4 × 5 oz. pieces rump steak
$\frac{1}{4}$ pint ($\frac{1}{2}$ cup + 2T) red wine
1 small onion, finely chopped
1 teaspoon mixed dried herbs
1 oz. (2T) lard or dripping
8 baby onions
1$\frac{1}{2}$ tablespoons (2T) flour

$\frac{1}{4}$ lb. carrots, sliced with a
   fluted chip cutter
salt
pepper
few drops of gravy browning
1 tablespoon (1$\frac{1}{4}$T) chopped
   parsley

Put the steak in a dish with the stock, wine, chopped onion and herbs and marinate for at least 2 hours, turning occasionally. Drain the meat, reserving the marinade. Melt the lard or dripping in a pan, add the meat and baby onions and fry until browned. Transfer to an ovenproof casserole.
Add the flour to the fat remaining in the pan and fry gently until browned. Stir in the marinade and bring to the boil. Add to the casserole with the carrots, seasoning and gravy browning. Cover and cook at 300°F, Gas Mark 2 for 1$\frac{1}{2}$ hours or until the meat is tender. Serve the meat in a hot dish with the vegetables arranged around it. Garnish with chopped parsley just before serving.
Serves 4

POT ROAST *(Photograph: Argentine Beef Bureau)*

Casseroled Oxtail

Queue de boeuf

3 lb. oxtail, in pieces
2 oz. ($\frac{1}{4}$ cup) lard or dripping
2 onions, chopped
2 large carrots, chopped
$\frac{1}{2}$ head of celery, chopped
2 rashers streaky bacon,
  chopped

2 tablespoons ($2\frac{1}{2}$T) flour
2 bay leaves
3 sprigs parsley
6 peppercorns
salt
2 pints (5 cups) beef stock
gravy browning

Trim off any excess fat from the oxtail joints. Heat the fat in a pan, add the oxtail and brown quickly on all sides, then remove from the pan. Add the vegetables and bacon to the pan and cook gently for 5 minutes. Blend in the flour, cook for 1 minute then return the oxtail to the pan with the remaining ingredients, except the gravy browning. Cover and simmer for 4 hours or until the meat can be removed easily from the bones. Arrange on a serving dish and keep hot.
Reduce the stock to $\frac{3}{4}$ pint (2 cups) by rapid boiling, check the seasoning, add a little gravy browning, then strain over the oxtail.
Serves 6

Madeira Sauce

Sauce madère

1 oz. (2T) butter
1 onion, sliced
1 carrot, sliced
$\frac{1}{2}$ pint ($1\frac{1}{4}$ cups) water
1 tablespoon ($1\frac{1}{4}$T) tomato
  purée
1 beef stock cube
2 sprigs parsley
1 sprig thyme

1 bay leaf
1 tablespoon ($1\frac{1}{4}$T) flour,
  blended with 2 tablespoons
  ($2\frac{1}{2}$T) water
1 tablespoon ($1\frac{1}{4}$T) redcurrant
  jelly
6 tablespoons ($7\frac{1}{2}$T) Madeira
  wine

Melt the butter in a pan, add the vegetables and cook slowly until soft. Add the water, tomato purée, stock cube and herbs and simmer for 20 minutes. Add the blended flour to the sauce and simmer until thickened. Stir in the redcurrant jelly and simmer until dissolved. Strain the sauce into a clean pan and add the Madeira. Re-heat before serving.

Kidneys in Wine

Rognons bordeaux

2 oz. ($\frac{1}{4}$ cup) butter
8 lamb's kidneys, skinned
   and halved
1 large onion, sliced
1 large carrot, sliced
1 tablespoon ($1\frac{1}{4}$T) flour
1 teaspoon tomato purée
$\frac{1}{2}$ pint ($1\frac{1}{4}$ cups) red Bordeaux
   wine

$\frac{1}{2}$ pint ($1\frac{1}{4}$ cups) beef stock
1 sprig of parsley
1 sprig of thyme
1 bay leaf
$\frac{1}{2}$ lb. ($2\frac{2}{3}$ cups) flat mushrooms
2 tablespoons ($2\frac{1}{2}$T) browned
   breadcrumbs
1 tablespoon ($1\frac{1}{4}$T) chopped
   parsley

Melt $1\frac{1}{2}$ oz. (3T) butter in a pan. Add the kidneys and brown quickly, then remove from the pan. Add the onion and carrot to the pan and fry until golden. Blend in the flour, cook for 1 minute, then add the purée, wine and stock. Bring to the boil, stirring. Replace the kidneys in the pan with the herbs, cover and simmer for 20 minutes.

Discard the herbs and turn the kidney mixture into a shallow ovenproof dish. Arrange the mushrooms on top, stalks uppermost. Sprinkle with breadcrumbs and brush with the remaining butter, which has been melted. Cook at 375°F, Gas Mark 5 for 15 minutes or until the top is browned. Sprinkle with parsley before serving.

Serves 4

Bayonne Lamb

Collier de mouton à la bayonne
A really economical French country stew.

2 lb. middle neck of lamb,
  chopped
2 onions, cut in wedges
2 large carrots, sliced
4 baby turnips, peeled and
  kept whole
1 bay leaf
1 tablespoon (1¼T) lemon
  juice
salt

pepper
2 pints (5 cups) water
¼ lb. (1⅓ cups) small
  mushrooms, sliced
1¼ oz. (3T) butter
1½ oz. (6T) flour
1 egg yolk
4 oz. carton (½ cup) thin
(coffee) cream

Put the lamb in a pan with the onions, carrots, turnips, bay leaf, lemon juice, seasoning and water. Bring to boiling point, cover and simmer for 1½ hours or until tender. Twenty minutes before the end of the cooking time add the mushrooms. Arrange the lamb and vegetables in a serving dish and keep hot.

Reduce the cooking liquor to 1 pint (2½ cups) by boiling rapidly. Make a roux with the butter and flour, add the cooking liquor and simmer for 5 minutes. Add more seasoning if necessary. Blend together the egg yolk and cream and add a little of the sauce. Return this mixture to the pan and re-heat but do not boil. Pour the sauce over the meat and vegetables.
Serves 4

Pepperpot Beef

Pot-au-feu piquant

1 oz. (4T) flour
1 teaspoon salt
$\frac{1}{8}$ teaspoon pepper
$\frac{1}{2}$ teaspoon ground ginger
2 lb. braising beef, in 1 inch
   cubes
2 oz. ($\frac{1}{4}$ cup) lard or dripping
1 small red pepper, sliced
15 oz. can red kidney beans,
   drained

Sauce:
1 teaspoon chilli sauce
8 oz. can tomatoes
$\frac{1}{4}$ lb. ($1\frac{1}{4}$ cups) mushrooms,
   sliced
1 tablespoon ($1\frac{1}{4}$T)
   Worcestershire sauce
2 tablespoons ($2\frac{1}{2}$T) soft brown
   sugar
2 tablespoons ($2\frac{1}{2}$T) wine
   vinegar
2 garlic cloves, crushed
1 bay leaf

Mix together the flour, seasonings and ginger and use to coat the beef. Heat the lard in a large pan, add the beef and fry quickly until browned, turning once. Drain on kitchen paper then transfer to a 3 pint ($8\frac{1}{2}$ cups) ovenproof dish.
Combine all the ingredients for the sauce and pour over the meat. Cover and cook at 325°F, Gas Mark 3 for about 2 hours or until the meat is tender. Add the red pepper and kidney beans 30 minutes before the end of the cooking time.
Serves 6

Pork Fillet in Wine

Filet de porc chasseur

2 lb. pork fillet (tenderloin)
2 tablespoons ($2\frac{1}{2}$T) oil
2 oz. (4T) butter
$\frac{1}{2}$ lb. onions, chopped
$\frac{1}{2}$ lb. ($2\frac{2}{3}$ cups) button
   mushrooms

2 tablespoons ($2\frac{1}{2}$T) flour
$\frac{1}{2}$ pint ($1\frac{1}{4}$ cups) beef stock
$\frac{1}{4}$ pint ($\frac{1}{2}$ cup) white wine
salt
pepper

Cut the pork in $1\frac{1}{2}$-inch pieces. Heat the oil in a pan, brown the pork quickly in the oil then remove from the pan. Heat the butter in the pan, add the onions and cook slowly until soft. Add the mushrooms.

Blend in the flour, stock and wine. Bring to the boil then simmer for 2-3 minutes. Replace the pork in the pan and season with salt and pepper. Cover and simmer for 40-50 minutes, until the pork is tender.

Serves 6

Pork in Cream Sauce

Côtelettes de porc à la crème

4 pork chops
salt
ground black pepper
$1\frac{1}{2}$ oz. (3T) butter
$\frac{1}{2}$ lb. ($2\frac{2}{3}$ cups) mushrooms, sliced

2 tablespoons ($2\frac{1}{2}$T) flour
$\frac{1}{2}$ pint ($1\frac{1}{4}$ cups) dry white wine
pinch dried mixed herbs
$\frac{1}{4}$ pint ($\frac{1}{2}$ cup + 2T) thin (coffee) cream

Season the chops with salt and pepper. Cook under a medium grill (broiler) for 10 minutes on a piece of foil, turning once, until crisp and brown. Save the juices on the foil. Place the chops on a serving dish and keep hot.

Melt the butter in a pan, add the mushrooms and fry gently for about 5 minutes until soft. Stir in the flour and cook for 1 minute. Blend in the juices from the foil, wine and herbs. Simmer for 2 minutes, stirring all the time. Add the cream and check the seasoning. Reheat almost to boiling point.

Pour the sauce over the chops. Serve with buttered noodles and grilled tomatoes.

Serves 4

Lamb in Pastry

Gigot d'agneau en croûte
This is a delicious way of cooking lamb. When you serve the joint, cut and lift the pastry off in portions and then carve the meat as you would normally. Serve with a rich gravy.

4 lb. leg of lamb
2 oz. ($\frac{1}{4}$ cup) butter
salt
pepper
For the pastry:
10 oz. ($2\frac{1}{2}$ cups) plain
   (all-purpose) flour

$\frac{3}{4}$ teaspoon salt
$2\frac{1}{2}$ oz. (5T) butter
$2\frac{1}{2}$ oz. (5T) lard
about 10 teaspoons water
Glaze:
1 egg, beaten with
1 teaspoon water

Have the bone of the joint cut short and trim off any excess fat. Rub the joint with the butter and sprinkle it with salt and pepper. Place it in the meat tin and roast it at 425°F, Gas Mark 7 for 75 minutes. Remove it from the oven and leave to cool. Sift the flour and salt into a bowl. Add the fats and rub in until the mixture resembles fine breadcrumbs. Add enough of the water to make a firm dough. Roll out the pastry to form a rectangle large enough to cover the lamb.
Wrap the lamb in the pastry with the joint underneath. Return the joint to the meat tin and decorate it with small leaves made from the pastry trimmings. Prick the pastry all over with a knife. Brush the pastry with beaten egg and bake the joint at 375°F, Gas Mark 5 for a further 45 minutes.
Serves 8

Veal Casserole

Blanquette de veau

$1\frac{1}{2}$ lb. boned shoulder veal,
   in $1\frac{1}{2}$ inch pieces
2 onions, quartered
2 large carrots, quartered
3 bay leaves
sprig of parsley
1 tablespoon ($1\frac{1}{4}$T) lemon juice
salt
pepper

2 pints (5 cups) water
6 oz. (2 cups) button
   mushrooms
$1\frac{1}{2}$ oz. (3T) butter
$1\frac{1}{2}$ oz. (6T) flour
1 egg yolk
$\frac{1}{4}$ pint ($\frac{1}{2}$ cup + 2T) thin
   (coffee) cream

Put the veal in a pan, cover with cold water and bring to the boil. Drain the veal and rinse off any scum. Put the veal pieces in a pan with the onions, carrots, bay leaves, parsley, lemon juice, seasoning and water. Bring to boiling point, cover and simmer for $1\frac{1}{2}$ hours or until the veal is tender. Half an hour before the end of the cooking time add the mushrooms. Arrange the veal and vegetables in a serving dish and keep hot.
Make a roux with the butter and flour. Reduce the cooking liquor to 1 pint ($2\frac{1}{2}$ cups) by boiling rapidly, then blend with the roux and simmer for 5 minutes. Check the seasoning. Blend together the egg yolk and cream. Add a little of the sauce. Return the egg mixture to the pan and re-heat but do not boil. Pour the sauce over the meat and vegetables.
Serves 4

Country Veal

Veau paysanne

4 veal chops
2 oz. ($\frac{1}{4}$ cup) lard or dripping
1 onion, stuck with a clove
rind and juice of $\frac{1}{2}$ a lemon
$\frac{1}{2}$ pint ($1\frac{1}{4}$ cups) dry cider
1 teaspoon arrowroot
salt
pepper
5 tablespoons ($6\frac{1}{4}$T) thin
   (coffee) cream off top of the
   milk

For the cabbage:
1 small white cabbage, finely
   shredded
1 oz. (2T) butter
1 onion, chopped
4 dessert apples, peeled,
   cored and quartered
juice of 1 lemon
salt
pepper
2 hard-boiled eggs, quartered
chopped parsley

Brown the chops in the fat, turning once. Pour off any surplus fat and add the onion, lemon rind and juice and cider. Cover and simmer gently until cooked, about 45 minutes.

Meanwhile, blanch the cabbage in boiling salted water about 1 minute, then drain well. Melt the butter in a pan, add the chopped onion and cook until softened. Add the cabbage and stir. Add the apple quarters and lemon juice to the cabbage. Add the seasoning, cover and simmer until tender, about 25 minutes.

Place the veal chops on a serving dish and keep hot. Strain the gravy from the chops onto the arrowroot, blended with a little cold water. Return to the pan and bring to the boil. Add seasoning. Simmer until thickened, remove from the heat and add cream, then spoon the sauce over the chops. Turn the cabbage into a hot dish, garnish with the eggs and parsley and serve with the chops.

Serves 4

Veal Birds

Paupiettes de veau
Chicken breasts, boned out and beaten, may be used instead of veal.

1 lb. veal fillet (scallops) in thin slices

2 rashers bacon, rinded and chopped

1 tablespoon (1¼T) chopped parsley

1 small garlic clove, crushed

2 oz. (1 cup) fresh white breadcrumbs

1 egg

1 oz. butter (2T)

1 tablespoon (1¼T) flour

¼ pint (½ cup + 2T) water or stock

¼ pint (½ cup + 2T) dry white wine

salt

pepper

¼ lb. (1⅓ cups) mushrooms, halved

4 tomatoes, peeled and quartered

few stuffed green olives

Beat the veal on a wooden board with a rolling pin until very thin. Mix together the bacon, parsley, garlic, breadcrumbs and egg and use to stuff the slices of veal. Roll each slice tightly and tie with fine string. Melt the butter in a pan, add the veal and fry quickly until browned. Remove the veal from the pan and place in a 2½ pint (6-cup) ovenproof dish.

Add the flour to the pan and cook for 1 minute. Stir in the water or stock and wine, bring to the boil, add seasoning and pour over the veal. Cover and cook at 325°F, Gas Mark 3 for 1 hour. Half an hour before the end of the cooking time add the remaining ingredients.

Serves 4

Chicken with Lemon Sauce

Poulet au citron

6 frying chicken joints
1 oz. (2T) butter
3 sprigs parsley
$\frac{1}{4}$ teaspoon dried thyme
thinly peeled rind and juice
  of 2 lemons
salt
pepper
$\frac{1}{2}$ pint (1$\frac{1}{4}$ cups) chicken stock

Garnish:
1 oz. (2T) lard

4 rashers streaky bacon,
  rinded and cut in strips
3 thick slices white bread

Sauce:
1$\frac{1}{2}$ oz. (3T) butter
1$\frac{1}{2}$ oz. (6T) flour
$\frac{1}{4}$ pint ($\frac{1}{2}$ cup + 2T) milk
salt
pepper

Remove the skin from the chicken joints. Put the joints in a meat tin, rounded side uppermost. Spread the butter on the joints, then add herbs and lemon rind. Sprinkle the joints with salt and pepper. Make lemon juice up to $\frac{1}{2}$ pint with stock then pour over the chicken. Cook, uncovered, at 400°F, Gas Mark 6 for about 30 minutes until tender, basting occasionally. Heat the lard in a frying pan, add the bacon and cook slowly until golden brown. Remove from the pan and drain on kitchen paper. Add the bread in $\frac{1}{4}$ inch cubes and fry until golden. Drain on kitchen paper and add to the bacon. Remove the chicken joints from the tin and keep hot. Strain the cooking liquor into a jug. Make a roux with the butter and flour. Cook for 2 minutes, then blend in the chicken, liquor and milk. Bring to boiling point, simmer for 2 to 3 minutes, stirring frequently. Add the seasoning, pour the sauce over the chicken and scatter the garnish on top.
Serves 6

Tarragon Chicken

Poulet à l'estragon

$3\frac{1}{2}$-4 lb. chicken
$\frac{1}{2}$ lemon
$\frac{1}{2}$ teaspoon salt
$\frac{1}{8}$ teaspoon pepper
$\frac{1}{4}$ teaspoon dried tarragon
3 carrots, quartered
1 onion, quartered
1 bay leaf
2 parsley sprigs
$\frac{3}{4}$ pint (2 cups) chicken stock
6 tablespoons ($7\frac{1}{2}$T) white wine

Sauce:
1 oz. (2T) butter
2 tablespoons ($2\frac{1}{2}$T) flour
$\frac{1}{2}$ teaspoon dried tarragon
2 egg yolks
5 tablespoons ($6\frac{1}{4}$T) thin
  (coffee) cream
salt
pepper

Put the chicken in a pan with the giblets and the first group
of ingredients. Cover and simmer for about $1\frac{1}{4}$ hours or until
tender. Remove the bird from the pan, skin and joint it and,
if liked, remove the bones. Keep the chicken hot.
Strain the cooking liquor into a measuring jug and make it up
to $\frac{3}{4}$ pint (2 cups) with water if necessary. Heat the butter in
a pan, blend in the flour and cook for 1 minute. Add the
chicken liquor and bring to the boil, stirring. Add the tarragon
and simmer for 3 minutes.
Blend together the egg yolks and cream. Add 4 tablespoons
(5T) sauce to the egg mixture then return it to the pan. Check
the seasoning, add the chicken pieces and heat through,
without simmering, for 5 minutes.
Serves 6

Chicken in Wine

Coq au vin

3-4 lb. boiling or roasting
   chicken
$1\frac{1}{2}$ oz. (3T) butter
1 tablespoon ($1\frac{1}{4}$T) salad oil
4 oz. piece smoked streaky
   bacon, cubed
12 baby onions
2 sticks celery, finely
   chopped
6 oz. (2 cups) mushrooms,
   quartered

1 garlic clove, crushed
2 tablespoons ($2\frac{1}{2}$T) flour
$\frac{3}{4}$ pint (2 cups) red Burgundy
$\frac{1}{4}$ pint ($\frac{1}{2}$ cup + 2T) water
1 bay leaf
1 sprig fresh thyme or
   $\frac{1}{4}$ teaspoon dried thyme
salt
pepper
the chicken giblets, washed
small triangles of fried bread

Wash and dry the chicken and cut into 6 joints. Melt 1 oz.
(2T) butter in a pan with the oil and fry the bacon cubes until
golden brown. Remove the bacon from the pan and drain on
kitchen paper. Fry the chicken until brown, turning once.
Put the joints, with the bacon, into a 3 pint (8 cup) ovenproof
casserole. Fry the onions with the celery in the fat remaining
in the pan until soft, then add to the casserole. Melt the
remaining butter in the pan, add the mushrooms and cook for
2 minutes, then put to one side, on kitchen paper.
Blend the garlic and flour with the fat remaining in the pan.
Cook gently until browned, stirring frequently. Add the wine,
water, herbs and seasoning to taste. Simmer until the mixture
has thickened. Pour over the chicken joints in the casserole
and add the giblets. Cover and cook at 325°F, Gas Mark 3 for
$1\frac{1}{2}$-4 hours, depending on the size of the bird and whether it
is a boiling or roasting chicken.
When almost tender remove the giblets and bay leaf from the
casserole. Stir in the mushrooms and cook for a further 10
minutes. Skim off any excess fat with absorbent kitchen paper.
Check the seasoning and garnish with fried bread triangles
before serving.
Serves 6

Pigeon Casserole with Chestnuts

Pigeons aux marrons

$\frac{3}{4}$ lb. chestnuts

3 plump pigeons, each split
  in half

3 tablespoons ($3\frac{3}{4}$T) oil

1 oz. (2T) butter

2 tablespoons ($2\frac{1}{2}$T) flour

$\frac{1}{2}$ pint ($1\frac{1}{4}$ cups) Beaujolais

$\frac{1}{2}$ pint ($1\frac{1}{4}$ cups) chicken stock

$\frac{1}{2}$ lb. onions, cut in wedges

thinly peeled rind and juice of
  1 orange

1 teaspoon redcurrant jelly

$\frac{1}{2}$ teaspoon salt

a bouquet garni

black pepper

parsley sprigs

Simmer the chestnuts in boiling water for about 2 minutes.
Drain, make a slit in each with a sharp knife and remove the
outer skin. Simmer for 20 minutes in water, then drain.
Heat 2 tablespoons ($2\frac{1}{2}$T) oil in a pan, add the butter then the
pigeons and fry until browned, turning once. Transfer the
birds to a 4 pint (10 cup) casserole. Add the remaining oil to
the pan with the chestnuts. Fry until evenly browned then
drain on kitchen paper.
Add the flour to the pan and cook gently until brown. Stir
in the wine and stock. Bring to the boil. Pour the sauce into
the casserole. Add all the other ingredients except the
chestnuts and parsley. Cover and cook at 325°F, Gas Mark 3
for about $1\frac{1}{2}$ to 2 hours or until tender. Add the chestnuts
about 45 minutes before the end of the cooking time. Remove
the bouquet garni and orange rind. Check the seasoning and
garnish with parsley sprigs before serving.
Serves 6

Rabbit Pie

Pâté chaud de lapin

Marinade:
$\frac{1}{2}$ pint ($1\frac{1}{4}$ cups) red wine
4 tablespoons (5T) olive oil
4 sprigs parsley
1 sprig thyme or
   $\frac{1}{4}$ teaspoon dried thyme
1 garlic clove, crushed
1 onion, chopped

Filling:
$1\frac{1}{2}$ lb. boned rabbit pieces
2 tablespoons ($2\frac{1}{2}$T) flour

1 teaspoon salt
$\frac{1}{8}$ teaspoon pepper
4 tablespoons (5T) oil
$\frac{1}{2}$ pint ($1\frac{1}{4}$ cups) chicken stock
few drops gravy browning
$\frac{1}{2}$ lb. baby onions
$\frac{1}{4}$ lb. piece of ham, cut in
   $\frac{1}{2}$ inch cubes

shortcrust pastry made with
   6 oz. flour, see page 26

Mix the ingredients for the marinade in a bowl. Add the
rabbit, cover and leave in a cold place for 12 hours, turning
occasionally. Drain the rabbit, reserving the marinade, and dry
on kitchen paper.
Mix together the flour, salt and pepper and use to coat the
rabbit pieces. Heat the oil in a pan, add the rabbit and fry
until golden brown. Add the marinade and stock, cover and
simmer for $1\frac{1}{2}$ hours, or until tender. Add the onions after 1
hour. Add a little gravy browning to give a rich colour. Put
the meat and cooking liquor in a 2 pint (5 cup) ovenproof dish
with the ham. Leave until cold.
Make the shortcrust pastry in the usual way, see page 26.
Use it to cover the pie dish. Chill for 15 minutes then bake at
400°F, Gas Mark 6 for 30 minutes or until golden brown.
Serves 6

Duck with Orange

Canard à l'orange

Watercress and an orange salad – sliced oranges in a dressing made from orange juice, wine vinegar and oil – are the classic accompaniments for this dish.

1 duckling, about 4½–5 lb.
salt
pepper
1 large orange
2 tablespoons (2½T) clear
  honey
few drops of gravy browning
1 oz. (4T) flour
¼ pint (½ cup + 2T) fresh
  orange juice

¼ pint (½ cup + 2T) red wine
1 tablespoon (1¼T) redcurrant
  jelly

Garnish:
1 orange, thinly sliced
bunch of watercress

Sprinkle the duckling inside and out with salt and pepper. Peel the zest from the orange and cut in thin strips. Discard the pith then divide the orange in segments. Put the segments in the body cavity of the duckling. Put in a meat tin and prick the entire body with a fork. Roast at 325°F, Gas Mark 3 for 2½–3 hours.

Cover the duck neck and giblets with water and cook until tender. Strain and reserve ½ pint (1¼ cups) stock.

Remove the duckling from the oven and raise the oven temperature to 350°F, Gas Mark 4. Pour off the dripping. Brush the duckling with the honey, mixed with gravy browning. Roast for a further 30 minutes.

Put 4 tablespoons (5T) dripping in a pan then blend in the flour. Stir in the stock, orange juice, wine and reserved strips of orange zest. Simmer until the sauce has reduced by a third. Add and dissolve the redcurrant jelly.

Put the duck on a hot serving dish. Spoon over a little of the sauce and serve the rest separately. Put the orange segments from the body cavity onto the breast of the duck and garnish with halved orange slices and sprigs of watercress.

Serves 4

Sauté of Cod

Cabillaud à la mistral

1 oz. (2T) butter
4 cod cutlets
1 onion, chopped
1 garlic clove, crushed
6 oz. (2 cups) mushrooms, sliced
$\frac{1}{2}$ lb. tomatoes, skinned, seeded and diced

5 tablespoons ($6\frac{1}{4}$T) dry white wine
salt
pepper
1 tablespoon ($1\frac{1}{4}$T) browned breadcrumbs
1 tablespoon ($1\frac{1}{4}$T) chopped parsley

Melt the butter in a frying pan, add the cod cutlets and cook gently for 10 minutes, turning once. Transfer the fish to a serving dish and keep hot.
Add the onion and garlic to the pan and cook slowly until the onion is soft but not coloured. Add the mushrooms and tomatoes and cook for a further 3 minutes. Stir in the wine, bring to the boil and simmer for 5 minutes. Check the seasoning and pour the sauce over the cutlets.
Mix together the breadcrumbs and parsley and scatter over the fish.
Serves 4

Fresh Salmon with Prawns

Saumon aux crevettes
A special summer dish.

$2\frac{1}{2}$ lb. tail piece salmon
$\frac{1}{4}$ pint ($\frac{1}{2}$ cup + 2T) dry white wine
$\frac{1}{2}$ pint ($1\frac{1}{4}$ cups) water
1 bay leaf
2 sprigs parsley
6 peppercorns

Garnish:
$1\frac{1}{2}$ teaspoons powdered gelatine
15 oz. can consommé
$\frac{1}{2}$ cucumber, thinly sliced
6 oz. ($\frac{3}{4}$ cup) shelled prawns (shrimps)

Put the salmon in a large buttered ovenproof dish with the other ingredients. Cover with a lid, or foil, and cook at 325°F, Gas Mark 3 for about 45 minutes, basting frequently. Remove from the oven and leave to cool in the dish, basting occasionally.

When cold remove the skin. Divide the fish in half by sliding a sharp knife along both sides of the flat backbone. Arrange on a large serving dish, putting a tail at each end of the dish. Put in the refrigerator.

Dissolve the gelatine with the consommé in a pan over gentle heat. Remove the pan from the heat and cool until the consommé has thickened slightly. Arrange the cucumber slices, overlapping slightly, round the edge of the salmon. Put the prawns in the centre, spoon the consommé over the top and chill until set.

Serves 6

Trout with Almonds

Truites aux amandes

2 oz. ($\frac{1}{4}$ cup) butter
2 oz. ($\frac{1}{3}$ cup) blanched
   almonds, shredded
4 trout, cleaned

salt
pepper
few parsley sprigs
4 black olives

Melt the butter in a frying pan, add the almonds and fry gently until golden brown. Remove the almonds from the pan. Meanwhile wash and dry the trout. Remove the fins and part of the tails but leave the heads on. Fry the trout in the butter remaining in the pan, allowing about 5 minutes on each side, according to size. Season to taste.

Arrange the trout on a hot serving dish with a black olive in the mouth of each. Sprinkle with the almonds and pour over the butter from the pan. Garnish with parsley.

Serves 4

Bacon and Onion Quiche

Quiche lorraine

4 oz. shortcrust pastry,
   see page 26

Filling:
1 small onion, chopped
$\frac{1}{2}$ oz. (1T) butter
$\frac{1}{4}$ lb. bacon, rinded

1 egg
$\frac{1}{4}$ pint ($\frac{1}{2}$ cup + 2T) thin
   (coffee) cream
salt
pepper
2 tomatoes, sliced

Use the pastry to line a 7 inch fluted flan ring placed on a
baking tray. Chill in the refrigerator for 10 minutes then bake
'blind' at 425°F, Gas Mark 7 for 15 minutes. Remove from the
oven and discard the paper and baking beans, or foil.
Fry the onion in the butter until soft but not coloured. Chop
the bacon and add to the pan. Fry the onion and bacon until
golden brown. Blend together the egg, cream and seasoning.
Put the onion and bacon in the flan case. Strain the egg
mixture on top. Arrange the tomatoes round the top of the
quiche. Cook at 350°F, Gas Mark 4 for 35 minutes or until the
filling is set.
Serves 4

SUPPORTING ROLES: VEGETABLES AND SALADS

In family meals in France and in restaurants which cater mainly for French customers rather than visiting tourists, vegetables or salads are served as a separate course. This enables one to savour the full flavour of the dish in isolation, a point worth remembering if the main course is itself highly flavoured. Among the recipes given here are one or two which could be served as a first course.

French Baked Onions

Oignons rôtis

8 large onions, peeled
2 oz. ($\frac{1}{4}$ cup) butter

salt
freshly ground black pepper

Dot the onions with butter, then season. Wrap each onion in foil and place on a baking tray. Bake at 350°F, Gas Mark 4 for about $1\frac{1}{2}$ hours, until tender.
Serves 4

Duchess Potatoes

Pommes de terre duchesse

1 lb. potatoes
1 egg yolk
1 oz. (2T) butter

salt
pepper
little beaten egg

Peel, boil and mash the potatoes. Beat in the egg yolk, butter and seasoning. Pipe in large rosettes on a baking tray. Brush with beaten egg and bake at 425°F, Gas Mark 7 until golden.

Country Fried Potatoes

Pommes de terre paysanne

1 lb. peeled potatoes   1 garlic clove, crushed
2 oz. ($\frac{1}{4}$ cup) butter

Cut the potatoes in $\frac{1}{2}$ inch dice. Fry gently in butter until golden brown. Add garlic to the pan just before serving and mix well.

Creamed Mushrooms

Champignons à la crème
Serve as a supper dish with a hot meaty soup.

3 large slices white bread, de-crusted
3 tablespoons ($3\frac{3}{4}$T) salad oil
1 lb. mushrooms, sliced
juice of 1 lemon
3 egg yolks, beaten
$\frac{1}{4}$ pint ($\frac{1}{2}$ cup + 2T) thin (coffee) cream

$\frac{1}{4}$ pint ($\frac{1}{2}$ cup + 2T) thick (heavy) cream
salt
pepper
4 rashers bacon grilled (broiled)

Cut the bread in $\frac{1}{4}$ inch dice, fry in oil until golden brown then drain on kitchen paper. Put the mushrooms in a pan with the lemon juice and sufficient water to cover. Bring to boiling point, simmer for 2 minutes then drain thoroughly.
Put the egg yolks blended with the creams in a bowl, over a pan of simmering water. Stir frequently, allowing the sauce to thicken. Add the mushrooms and seasoning.
Turn into a shallow, heated dish and top with croûtons and bacon.
Serves 4

Lyonnaise Potatoes

Pommes de terre lyonnaise

1 lb. potatoes, peeled and thinly sliced	2 oz. ($\frac{1}{4}$ cup) butter salt
1 large onion, thinly sliced	pepper chopped parsley

Blanch the potatoes in boiling water for 1 minute, then drain. Fry the onion in butter for a few minutes, without colouring. Layer the onion, potatoes and seasoning in a buttered 2 pint (5 cup) casserole, finishing with a layer of potatoes. Pour over any butter left in the pan, cover and bake at 400°F, Gas Mark 6 for $1\frac{1}{2}$ hours. Remove the lid for the last 30 minutes to allow the potatoes to brown. Sprinkle with parsley.

Courgette (Zucchini) Fritters

Beignets de courgettes
Serve as a starter with tomato sauce, or as a vegetable.

1 lb. courgettes (zucchini)	$\frac{1}{2}$ teaspoon salt
	2 eggs, separated
Batter:	about $\frac{1}{4}$ pint
4 oz. (1 cup) plain (all-purpose) flour	($\frac{1}{2}$ cup + 2T) milk oil for deep frying

Cut the courgettes in $\frac{1}{4}$ inch slices. Put the flour and salt in a bowl and blend in the egg yolks. Add sufficient milk to make a coating batter. Whisk the egg whites stiffly and fold into the batter.

Heat the oil in a pan, dip the sliced courgettes in the batter then fry until golden brown. Drain on kitchen paper and serve hot.
Serves 4

Braised Chicory

Endives braisés
In France chicory is endive and endive is chicory – all very muddling.
Chicory is often thought to be rather bitter when cooked. I find it best to
braise it, adding a little sugar.

$1\frac{1}{2}$ lb. chicory
1 oz. (2T) butter
3 tablespoons ($3\frac{3}{4}$T) water
1 teaspoon lemon juice
1 teaspoon castor (superfine)
  sugar

$\frac{1}{2}$ teaspoon salt
$\frac{1}{8}$ teaspoon freshly ground
  black pepper

Put the chicory in a pan of boiling water and boil for 2
minutes. Drain in a colander and rinse with cold water.
Butter a 2 pint (5 cup) shallow ovenproof dish with half of the
butter. Arrange the chicory in the dish. Add the remaining
ingredients and dot with the remaining butter. Cover with a
piece of greaseproof paper, then a lid. Cook at 300°F, Gas Mark
2 for 1-$1\frac{1}{4}$ hours until tender.
Lift carefully from the pan and serve with the juices from the
dish.
Serves 4

Chicory with Cheese

Endives au gratin

$1\frac{1}{2}$ oz. (3T) butter
8 small heads of chicory,
  quartered lengthways
juice of 1 lemon
1 teaspoon castor (superfine)
  sugar
$\frac{1}{4}$ teaspoon salt

pinch of pepper

Cheese topping:
2 oz. ($\frac{1}{2}$ cup) Cheddar cheese,
  grated
1 oz. ($\frac{1}{4}$ cup) Parmesan cheese,
  grated

Use $\frac{1}{2}$ oz. (1T) butter to grease a shallow $1\frac{1}{2}$ pint (4 cup) ovenproof casserole. Add chicory and lemon juice and turn well to coat with lemon. Dot with the remaining butter and add sugar and seasoning. Cover tightly and cook at 350°F, Gas Mark 4 for about 45 minutes or until tender. Baste once or twice while cooking.

Clean the sides of the dish with a hot moist cloth. Sprinkle with cheese and return to the oven to brown for a further 30 minutes.

Serves 4

Hollandaise Sauce

Sauce hollandaise

2 tablespoons ($2\frac{1}{2}$T) wine
  vinegar
2 tablespoons ($2\frac{1}{2}$T) lemon
  juice
2 bay leaves
2 blades mace

6 peppercorns
3 egg yolks
4 oz. ($\frac{1}{2}$ cup) butter
salt
pepper

Put the vinegar, lemon juice, bay leaves, mace and pepper-corns into a small pan and simmer until the liquor has reduced to 2 tablespoons ($2\frac{1}{2}$T). Put the egg yolks into a small bowl, blend in the strained liquor from the pan and mix well.

Put the bowl on top of a pan of hot, *not* boiling water. Beat in a knob of soft butter and then whisk the mixture over the heat until it has thickened. Gradually add the remaining butter. Whisk constantly and remove the bowl from the heat if the sauce thickens too quickly. When finished the sauce should form very soft peaks. Add salt and pepper to taste. Keep the sauce warm by standing it in a bowl over warm, not hot, water until required.

Serves 4

Asparagus

Asperges

1 lb. bundle of asparagus   salt

Trim off the white and brown jagged ends of the asparagus and cut all the sticks to an average length. Scrape off the rough skin near the cut end with a sharp knife. Wash well in cold water.
Bring a large, shallow pan of salted water to the boil, add the asparagus, cover and simmer for 12 to 15 minutes or until just tender. Lift out the asparagus carefully and drain.
Serve hot with hollandaise sauce, see previous page, or melted butter, or cold with French dressing, see page 64.
Serves 2-3

Leeks with Cheese

Poireaux au gratin

4 leeks	$\frac{1}{2}$ pint ($1\frac{1}{4}$ cups) milk
salt	3 oz. ($\frac{3}{4}$ cup)
1 oz. (2T) butter	grated cheese
2 tablespoons ($2\frac{1}{2}$T) flour	pepper

Trim the roots and green part from the leeks. Wash very thoroughly, then cook in boiling salted water for 10 minutes or until just tender. Drain and arrange in a shallow 2 pint (5 cup) ovenproof dish, reserving 4 tablespoons (5T) cooking liquor.
Make a roux with the butter and flour, blend in the milk and reserved cooking liquor and bring to boiling point, stirring. Add most of the cheese and season well. Pour the sauce over the leeks and sprinkle with the remaining cheese. Cook under a medium grill (broiler) for about 5 minutes.
Serves 4

62   ASPARAGUS

Potato and Celery Salad

Salade de pommes de terre et céleri

1 lb. potatoes
salt
6 tablespoons (7½T) French
  dressing
1 small head of celery,
  chopped
2 large, sweet gherkins, sliced

¼ pint (½ cup + 2T)
  mayonnaise, see opposite
salt
pepper
1 tablespoon (1¼T) chopped
  chives

Boil the potatoes in salted water in the usual way then drain,
toss in French dressing and leave until cold.
Slice the potatoes into a bowl, add the celery, gherkins and
mayonnaise and season well. Add most of the chives then
cover and leave in a cool place until required. Sprinkle with
the remaining chives before serving.
Serves 4-6

French Dressing

Sauce vinaigrette

½ garlic clove, crushed
½ teaspoon dry mustard
½ teaspoon salt
½ teaspoon freshly ground
  black pepper
1 teaspoon very finely
  chopped onion or a few
  finely chopped chives

1 teaspoon castor (superfine)
  sugar
¼ pint (½ cup + 2T) olive,
  vegetable or corn oil
4-6 tablespoons (5-7½T) white
  wine vinegar or cider
  vinegar (or half each
  vinegar and lemon juice)

Blend the first six ingredients together in a bowl. Mix in the
oil slowly with a whisk or spoon. Finally stir in the vinegar
or vinegar and lemon juice. Taste and adjust the seasoning if
necessary.

For a simpler French dressing that will keep, omit the chives or onion and lemon juice. Put all the ingredients together in a screw-top jar, replace the lid and shake vigorously until well blended. In this way, the ingredients can be proportionately increased and more made at one time. The dressing can be kept in the jar in a cool place for up to six weeks.

Mayonnaise

2 egg yolks
$\frac{1}{2}$ teaspoon made mustard
$\frac{1}{2}$ teaspoon salt
$\frac{1}{8}$ teaspoon freshly ground black pepper
$\frac{1}{2}$ teaspoon castor (superfine) sugar

$\frac{1}{2}$ pint ($1\frac{1}{4}$ cups) olive, vegetable or corn oil
1 tablespoon ($1\frac{1}{4}$T) lemon juice
1 tablespoon ($1\frac{1}{4}$T) white wine vinegar or cider vinegar

Stand a bowl on a damp cloth to prevent it from slipping on the table. Put in the egg yolks, mustard, salt, pepper and sugar. Mix thoroughly, then add the oil drop by drop, beating well with a whisk the whole time, until the sauce is thick and smooth. Beat in the vinegar and lemon juice. This makes a thick, traditional mayonnaise. Add a little thin cream or top of the milk for a thinner mixture.

Should the sauce curdle through adding the oil too quickly to the egg yolks, take a fresh egg yolk and begin again, adding the curdled mayonnaise very slowly in the same way as the oil is added to the original egg yolks.

Aioli Sauce

Sauce Aïoli

2 or 3 garlic cloves, crushed
3 egg yolks
$\frac{1}{3}$ pint (scant 1 cup)
   vegetable or nut oil

$\frac{1}{2}$ teaspoon salt
$\frac{1}{2}$ teaspoon pepper
2 tablespoons ($2\frac{1}{2}$T)
   lemon juice

Blend the garlic and egg yolks in a bowl. Gradually whisk in
the oil as for mayonnaise. Stir in the seasoning and lemon
juice. Serve as a dip with fresh pieces of raw vegetables.

Vegetables Aioli

Aïoli

Aïoli, see above
$\frac{1}{2}$ small white cabbage,
   finely shredded

4 oz. salami, cut in pieces
2 oz. black olives
4 hard-boiled eggs, quartered

Make the aïoli as above.
Arrange the cabbage on a serving dish. Top with the salami,
olives and egg quarters. Pour over the aïoli sauce just before
serving.
Serves 4

INTERMISSION: CAKES AND PASTRIES

No book on French cooking would be complete without a section on cakes and pastries, those mouth-watering delicacies which adorn the windows of *patisseries* throughout the country. If you want to be popular with your friends, try offering them any of the following recipes, but for kindness's sake, don't invite those on a diet.

Little Nun Cakes

Les petites religieuses

Choux pastry
$\frac{1}{4}$ pint ($\frac{1}{2}$ cup + 2T) milk
  and water, mixed
$1\frac{1}{2}$ oz. (3T) butter
pinch of salt
$2\frac{1}{2}$ oz. ($\frac{1}{2}$ cup + 2T) plain
  (all-purpose) flour
2 eggs
Pastry cream:
2 eggs
2 oz. ($\frac{1}{4}$ cup) castor
  (superfine) sugar
1 oz. (2T) plain
  (all-purpose) flour
$\frac{1}{2}$ pint ($1\frac{1}{4}$ cups) milk
few drops vanilla essence

Chocolate glacé icing:
2 oz. (2 squares) plain
  chocolate
nob of butter
6 oz. (1 cup + 2T) icing
  (confectioners') sugar, sifted
water

Chocolate butter icing:
$1\frac{1}{2}$ oz. (3T) butter
3 oz. ($\frac{1}{2}$ cup) icing
  (confectioners') sugar, sifted
1 oz. (1 square) plain
  chocolate, melted

Put the milk and water, butter and salt into a pan. Heat gently until the butter has melted then bring to the boil. Remove from the heat, add the flour and stir until smooth. Cook for 1 minute, stirring. Cool the mixture slightly, then gradually beat in the eggs. Beat until the mixture leaves the sides of the pan. Put the paste into a large piping bag fitted with a $\frac{1}{2}$ inch plain pipe. Dampen some baking trays. Pipe 9 balls of $1\frac{1}{2}$ inch diameter and 9 balls of $\frac{1}{2}$ inch diameter. Bake at 400°F, Gas Mark 6 for 25-30 minutes until crisp and golden. Make a slit in each bun so the steam can escape. Cool on a wire rack. Whisk the egg yolks with the sugar for the pastry cream until pale. Blend in the flour and a little of the milk. Boil the rest of the milk then pour on to the egg mixture, stirring well. Return to the pan and cook for 2-3 minutes, stirring. Cool slightly. Whisk the egg whites until stiff then fold into the pastry cream with the vanilla essence. When cold, use to fill the choux buns. Melt the chocolate with the butter for the glacé icing in a bowl placed over a pan of hot water. When melted, stir in the icing (confectioners') sugar. Add just enough water to make a thick glacé icing. Use to coat the top of the large buns. Place a small bun on top of each and coat with icing. Leave to set.

Beat together all the ingredients for the butter icing. Leave in a cold place until stiff enough to pipe. Using a small rose pipe and a forcing bag, pipe rosettes of chocolate butter-cream round the bases of each small bun to give a wreath effect.
Makes 9

Florentines

2 oz. ($\frac{1}{4}$ cup) butter
2 oz. ($\frac{1}{4}$ cup) castor
  (superfine) sugar
2 oz. ($\frac{1}{3}$ cup) mixed walnuts
  and almonds, chopped finely
$\frac{1}{2}$ oz. (1T) candied peel,
  chopped

$\frac{1}{2}$ oz. (1T) glacé cherries,
  chopped
$\frac{1}{2}$ oz. (1T) sultanas, chopped
1 tablespoon ($1\frac{1}{4}$T) thin
  (coffee) cream
3 oz. (3 squares) plain
  chocolate, melted

Melt the butter in a pan, then add the sugar. Boil for 1 minute. Add nuts, peel, cherries and sultanas to pan with the cream. Grease 2 or 3 baking trays well. Put teaspoons of the mixture on the baking trays, allowing plenty of room for them to spread. Bake at 350°F, Gas Mark 4 for 10 minutes or until deep golden brown. Remove from the oven and press into shape with a palette knife. Allow to cool slightly before lifting on to a wire rack to cool.

Spread melted chocolate over the backs of the florentines with a palette knife. Make wavy patterns with a fork. Leave to set.
Makes about 20

Brioches

3 tablespoons ($3\frac{3}{4}$T) water
$\frac{1}{2}$ oz. (2 teaspoons) dried yeast
$\frac{1}{2}$ teaspoon castor (superfine) sugar
8 oz. (2 cups) plain (all-purpose) flour
$\frac{1}{2}$ teaspoon salt
$\frac{1}{2}$ oz. (1T) castor (superfine) sugar

2 eggs, beaten
2 oz. ($\frac{1}{4}$ cup) butter, melted and cooled

Egg glaze:
1 egg
1 tablespoon ($1\frac{1}{4}$T) cold water, pinch of sugar, all blended together

Grease twelve 3-inch brioche tins well, or use deep fluted patty (muffin) tins. Heat the water until lukewarm and pour into a small bowl. Whisk in the yeast and $\frac{1}{2}$ teaspoon castor (superfine) sugar. Leave in a warm place for about 10 minutes, until the yeast has dissolved and froth appears.

Sift the flour and salt into a bowl. Mix in the remaining sugar. Stir in the yeast mixture, eggs and butter. Beat by hand until the mixture leaves the sides of the bowl. Knead on a lightly floured board for 5 minutes. Place the dough in a slightly oiled polythene bag and leave to rise at room temperature until it has doubled in size and springs back when lightly pressed with a finger – this takes about $1\frac{1}{2}$ hours.

Knead well on a lightly floured board for about 5 minutes. Divide the dough in 4 equal pieces, then each piece in 3. With each piece, use about $\frac{3}{4}$ to form a ball. Place the balls of dough in tins and firmly press a hole in the centre. Place the remaining small piece of dough in the hole.

Place the tins on a baking tray. Cover with a large, oiled polythene bag. Leave to rise in a warm place until light and puffy, about 1 hour. Brush lightly with egg glaze. Bake at 450°F, Gas Mark 8 for about 10 minutes. Serve warm.
Makes 12

Dark Chocolate Cake

Gâteau au chocolat

$2\frac{1}{2}$ oz. ($\frac{1}{2}$ cup + 2T) self-
  raising (all-purpose) flour

$\frac{1}{2}$ oz. (2T) cocoa

4 oz. (4 squares) plain
  chocolate

4 oz. ($\frac{1}{2}$ cup) butter

4 oz. ($\frac{1}{2}$ cup) castor
  (superfine) sugar

4 eggs, separated

Filling:
4 rounded tablespoons (5T)
  apricot jam

1 tablespoon ($1\frac{1}{4}$T) water

Icing:
6 oz. (good cup) icing
  (confectioners') sugar,
  sieved

$\frac{1}{2}$ oz. (2T) cocoa

2 oz. ($\frac{1}{4}$ cup) butter

2 oz. (2 squares) plain
  chocolate

2 tablespoons ($2\frac{1}{2}$T) milk

Line an 8 inch cake tin with greased greaseproof paper. Sift together the flour and cocoa. Melt the chocolate in a small bowl over a pan of simmering water, remove from the heat then cool.

Beat the butter and sugar until pale and creamy. Beat in the egg yolks one at a time, beating well after each addition. Fold in the flour mixture alternately with the melted chocolate. Whisk the egg whites until they form soft peaks, fold into the cake mixture. Turn into the prepared tin, bake at 350°F, Gas Mark 4 for about 50 minutes or until a skewer inserted in the centre comes out clean. Turn the cake out on a wire rack to cool. Cut in three layers when cold.

Put the filling ingredients in a pan, bring to the boil and simmer for 1 minute, then sieve. Brush the cut surfaces of the cake with half the filling. Reassemble on the wire rack. Brush the top and sides of the cake with remaining filling.

Sift together the icing sugar and cocoa for the icing. Heat the remaining ingredients together gently in a pan until the butter and chocolate have melted. Remove from the heat, add the sifted ingredients and beat until thick. Spread the icing quickly over the cake and leave in a cool place to become firm.

Basque Cake

Gâteau Basque
Serve Gâteau Basque for dessert or at tea time

Pastry cream:
2 egg yolks
2 oz. ($\frac{1}{4}$ cup) castor
　(superfine) sugar
$\frac{1}{2}$ pint ($1\frac{1}{4}$ cups) milk

2 tablespoons ($2\frac{1}{2}$T)
　cornflour (cornstarch)
1 egg white
few drops of vanilla essence

Beat together the egg yolks, one teaspoon of the sugar, the cornflour (cornstarch) and sufficient milk to make a smooth paste. Boil the remaining milk, pour on to the egg mixture and return to the pan. Simmer until thickened then remove from the heat.

Whisk the egg white until stiff then whisk in the remaining sugar and vanilla essence. Fold in to the boiled mixture and leave until cold.

Pastry:
12 oz. (3 cups) self-raising
　(all-purpose) flour
2 oz. ($\frac{1}{2}$ cup) cornflour
　(cornstarch)
6 oz. ($\frac{3}{4}$ cup) butter
8 oz. (1 cup) castor (superfine)
　sugar

2 eggs
1 egg yolk
grated rind of 1 lemon
about 1 tablespoon ($1\frac{1}{4}$T)
　lemon juice or brandy

Sift together the flour and cornflour (cornstarch). Cream the butter and sugar until soft then add the eggs and yolk, together with the lemon rind. Work in the flour and enough lemon juice or brandy to give a soft rolling consistency. Cover and chill for 30 minutes.

Use half the pastry to line the base and sides of an 11 inch loose-bottomed fluted flan tin. Press the pastry into place with the fingers as it is very soft. Spread the pastry cream on top. Cover with the remaining pastry. Bake at 350°F, Gas Mark 4 for about 45 minutes or until the pastry is golden brown.
Serves about 10

Magali

2 oz. ($\frac{1}{4}$ cup) butter
2 oz. ($\frac{1}{4}$ cup) castor
  (superfine) sugar
few drops of vanilla essence
4 oz. (1 cup) plain
  (all-purpose) flour
3 oz. (3 squares) plain
  chocolate

1 egg yolk
$\frac{1}{2}$ oz. (1T) unsalted butter
4 tablespoons (5T) thick
  (heavy) cream
2 teaspoons rum or fruit
  squash
6 oz. (1 cup + 2T) icing
  (confectioners') sugar

Grease about 18 individual, fairly shallow patty (muffin) tins.
Cream the butter and sugar together until lighter in colour,
add the vanilla essence and egg yolk. Work the flour into the
mixture. Roll out the pastry thinly on a floured board and use
to line the patty tins. Prick the bases with a fork, then bake at
375°F, Gas Mark 5 for 10-15 minutes until golden brown.
Remove from the tins and cool on a wire rack.
Melt the chocolate, butter and cream in a pan over gentle heat,
stirring continuously. Remove from the heat, add rum and
allow to cool completely, beating occasionally until thick.
Divide between the pastry cases. Add enough water to the
icing (confectioners') sugar to make a thick glacé icing. Spoon
over the chocolate mixture and decorate with a chocolate curl
or piece of flaked chocolate bar. Leave to set.
Makes 18

MAGALI *(Photograph: Cadbury Schweppes Food Advisory Service, Bournville, Birmingham, England)*

Most French families finish their meals with fresh fruit and cheese, but even when special desserts are served the dish is usually fairly light. French schoolchildren visiting Britain go overboard for rolypoly and suet pudding but this is because they have no equivalent at home. In this chapter, I have concentrated on delicate, rich dishes which the French do so well.

Apricot and Orange Cream

Crème aux abricots et oranges
A smooth fruit cream with a refreshing taste.

1 lb. apricots
4 oz. ($\frac{1}{2}$ cup) sugar
$\frac{1}{4}$ pint ($\frac{1}{2}$ cup + 2T) water
grated rind and juice of 2
   large oranges

$\frac{1}{2}$ oz. (1T) powdered gelatine
$\frac{1}{2}$ pint (1$\frac{1}{4}$ cups)
   thick (heavy) cream
$\frac{1}{2}$ teaspoon Demerara (raw)
   sugar

Stew the apricots in the sugar and water.
Puree the apricots with the syrup in a blender or put through a sieve. Stir in the orange rind and juice of 1 orange.
Put the remaining orange juice with the gelatine in a small bowl placed over a pan of simmering water. Leave until the gelatine has dissolved, then stir into apricot mixture and cool. Whip all but 3 tablespoons (3$\frac{3}{4}$T) cream until soft peaks are formed. When the apricot mixture begins to thicken, fold in the cream.
Pour into a 1$\frac{1}{2}$ pint (4 cup) glass dish and leave in a cold place until set. Just before serving, pour over the remaining cream and sprinkle with the sugar.
Serves 6

Cream Caramel

Crème caramel

Do not worry if the custard takes longer to cook than the time given. It will set eventually. Do not increase the oven temperature or the custard will boil and curdle and when finished it will have an unpleasant texture.

Caramel:
3 oz. (6 tablespoons) castor
   (superfine) sugar
3 tablespoons ($3\frac{3}{4}$T) water

Custard:
4 eggs
1 pint ($2\frac{1}{2}$ cups) milk
$1\frac{1}{2}$ oz. (3T) castor (superfine)
   sugar
few drops vanilla essence

Put the sugar and the water for the caramel in a heavy pan over a very low heat. Allow the sugar to dissolve slowly, without boiling. Bring the syrup to the boil and keep boiling until pale golden brown, then pour quickly into the base of a $1\frac{1}{2}$ pint (4 cup) charlotte mould or cake tin.

Blend together, using a fork, the eggs, sugar and vanilla essence in a bowl. Warm the milk in a pan until hand hot, then pour on to egg mixture, stirring well.

Butter the sides of the mould or tin above the caramel. Strain the custard into the mould or tin and place in a meat tin half filled with hot water. Bake at 300°F, Gas Mark 2 for about $1\frac{1}{2}$ hours or until a knife inserted in the centre comes out clean. Remove the custard from oven and leave to become completely cold, at least 12 hours or overnight, before turning out on to a flat dish just before serving.

Serves 4

Fruit and Cheese Dessert

Le fromage et les fruits

Serve a selection of French cheeses such as Camembert and Brie with iced melon balls, black grapes, radishes, stuffed olives and pears. They look beautiful arranged on vine leaves with a bunch of green grapes. If no vine leaves are available use blackcurrant leaves.

Floating Islands

Iles flottantes

$1\frac{1}{2}$ pints ($3\frac{3}{4}$ cups) milk
few drops of vanilla essence
3 eggs, separated

5 oz. ($\frac{1}{2}$ cup + 2T) castor
  (superfine) sugar
few fresh strawberries

Heat the milk to simmering point in a large pan. Add the vanilla essence. Whisk 2 egg whites until stiff then whisk in 4 oz. ($\frac{1}{2}$ cup) of sugar a teaspoon at a time, whisking well after each addition.
Place tablespoons of meringue on top of the milk and poach for 10 minutes, until set. Place meringue 'islands' on a plate. Strain the milk and measure 1 pint ($2\frac{1}{2}$ cups). Beat together the egg yolks, remaining egg and remaining sugar. Pour on the measured milk, return to the pan and heat gently, without simmering, until thickened.
Strain the custard into a large shallow dish. Lay the 'islands' on top and serve with fresh strawberries. Serve warm or cold.
Serves 4

FRUIT AND CHEESE *(Photograph: Fruit Producers' Council)*

Almond Ice Cream

Glace praliné
An easy ice-cream to make and richly flavoured with almonds and caramel.

Praline:
2 oz. ($\frac{1}{4}$ cup) castor
   (superfine) sugar
2 tablespoons ($2\frac{1}{2}$T) water
2 oz. ($\frac{1}{3}$ cup) unblanched
   almonds

Ice cream:
4 eggs, separated
4 oz. ($\frac{3}{4}$ cup) icing
   (confectioners') sugar,
   sifted
$\frac{1}{2}$ pint ($1\frac{1}{4}$ cups) thick (heavy)
   cream, lightly whipped

Put the castor (superfine) sugar and water in a pan, heat slowly
until the sugar has dissolved then add the almonds. Cook
quickly until mixture is a deep golden brown, stirring
frequently.
Turn on to an oiled baking tray. Leave until set then
pulverise in a blender or put praline between a double layer
of greaseproof paper and crush with a rolling pin.
Whisk the egg yolks until blended. In another bowl whisk the
whites until stiff then whisk in the icing (confectioners') sugar
a teaspoon at a time, making a meringue. Whisk the egg yolks
into the meringue mixture with the cream. Turn into a $2\frac{1}{2}$
pint plastic container, cover and freeze for 2 hours.
Turn the mixture into a bowl, whisk until smooth, then stir
in the praline. Return to the freezer in a covered container and
freeze until required.
Serves 8

Pineapple Sorbet

Sorbet a l'ananas

1 medium sized fresh
   pineapple
juice of $1\frac{1}{2}$ lemons

$\frac{3}{4}$ pint (scant 2 cups) water
6 oz. ($\frac{3}{4}$ cup) castor
   (superfine) sugar

Cut the pineapple in half lengthways, cut out the hard core down the centre of each side. Keep the pineapple shells. With a grapefruit knife or sharply pointed spoon, scoop out all the flesh and chop finely, saving the juice. Mix the chopped pineapple, juice and lemon juice together. Put the water and sugar in a pan over low heat. Allow the sugar to dissolve slowly, then cool. This makes a thin syrup.

Add the sugar syrup to pineapple, pour into freezer trays or shallow plastic containers – the total liquid is about $1\frac{1}{2}$ pints ($3\frac{3}{4}$ cups). Freeze in the refrigerator freezing compartment, set to coldest, or in the freezer until the mixture is set but not hard.

Turn the sorbet into a bowl and whisk until broken up and light. Re-freeze, having covered the trays or containers with foil or lids.

Scoop out with a metal spoon that has been dipped in boiling water, and serve in the pineapple shells.

Serves 6

Fresh Fruit Salad

Salade de fruits

1 large pineapple
2 dessert apples, cored and sliced
2 pears, peeled, cored and sliced

2 oranges, peeled and sliced
4 oz. jar maraschino cherries, drained
castor (superfine) sugar
1 tablespoon ($1\frac{1}{4}$T) Cointreau

Cut the top from the pineapple. Scoop out the flesh, leaving a wall about $\frac{1}{4}$ inch thick. Discard the core and cut the flesh in small pieces.

Put in a bowl with the apple, pear and orange slices. Add the cherries and sprinkle with sugar to taste. Add the liqueur, cover and leave in a cool place until the sugar has dissolved. Stand the pineapple upright and pile the fruit into it. Any remaining fruit salad may be offered separately.

Serves 6-8

Blackcurrant Sorbet

Sorbet au cassis

15 oz. can blackcurrants
6 oz. (¾ cup) granulated
   sugar
grated rind and juice of
   1 lemon

1 teaspoon powdered gelatine
1 tablespoon (1¼T) water
2 egg whites

Drain the blackcurrants, reserving the juice. Make the juice up to ¾ pint (2 cups) with water and put it in a pan with the sugar. Heat gently until the sugar has dissolved, stirring occasionally. Simmer for 2 minutes, remove from the heat and add the lemon rind and juice.

Dissolve the gelatine with the water in a bowl over a pan of simmering water. Sieve the blackcurrants then stir the purée into the sugar syrup with the gelatine. Turn the mixture into a plastic container, cover it and leave in the freezing compartment of the refrigerator, or in the deep-freeze until almost frozen. Put the mixture in a bowl and whisk until smooth. Whisk the egg whites until they form soft peaks, fold into the blackcurrant mixture. Return to the plastic container, cover and freeze until required. Serve with Cigarette Biscuits (see page 84).

Serves 6

Cigarettes

2 egg whites
$3\frac{1}{2}$ oz. (scant $\frac{1}{2}$ cup)
  castor (superfine) sugar
$1\frac{1}{2}$ oz. (6T) plain (all-purpose)
  flour, sifted

2 oz. ($\frac{1}{4}$ cup) butter, melted
  and cooled

Grease 2 or 3 baking trays. Whisk the egg whites until stiff. Fold in the sugar, then the flour. Lastly fold in the melted butter. Stir as little as possible. Put teaspoons of the mixture on baking trays and spread each thinly, to a 3 inch circle. Bake at 400°F, Gas Mark 6 for 4-5 minutes.
When golden round the edges, remove one at a time from the baking tray with a sharp knife. Wrap quickly round a pencil or a wooden spoon handle. This must be done quickly or the cigarettes will harden and crack when rolled. Remove from the pencil or spoon when firm, then cool. Store in an airtight tin. Serve with ice cream or at tea-time.
Makes about 30

Cream Cheese Hearts

Coeurs à la crème
This is best served well chilled, with extra cream. Both fresh strawberries and raspberries are delicious with it.

two 8 oz. cartons (2 cups)
  cottage cheese
5 oz. carton ($\frac{1}{2}$ cup + 2T)
  soured cream

2 tablespoons ($2\frac{1}{2}$T) icing
  (confectioners') sugar, sifted
$\frac{1}{4}$ teaspoon salt

Sieve the cottage cheese, or purée in a blender. Beat the cream, sugar and salt until smooth. Blend in the cheese.
Turn the mixture into four 6 oz. ($\frac{3}{4}$ cup) moulds, preferably heart-shaped and lined with a double thickness of damp muslin. Pack the mixture tightly into the moulds, squeeze

the liquid out through the muslin. Pour off the liquid from inside the mould. Squeeze frequently. Chill overnight in the refrigerator.

Unmould onto a plate, remove the muslin and serve with fresh strawberries, sugar and thick (heavy) cream.

Serves 8

Fruit Fritters

Beignets de fruits

7 oz. (1¾ cups) plain
  (all-purpose) flour
1 oz. (2T) castor (superfine)
  sugar
⅜ pint (1 cup) white wine
1 tablespoon (1¼T)
  olive oil
grated rind of ½ lemon
3 eggs, separated
3 dessert apples, peeled, cored
  and finely chopped

1 oz. (2T) dried apricots,
  finely chopped
1 oz. (2T) sultanas
1½ oz. (¼ cup) blanched
  almonds, finely chopped
1 tablespoon (1¼T) rum
oil for deep frying
extra castor (superfine) sugar

Put the flour and sugar in a bowl. Make a well in the centre and pour in the wine, olive oil and lemon rind. Mix well then beat in the egg yolks. Leave the batter in a cool place until required.

Put the apples, apricots, sultanas and almonds in a bowl with the rum and leave to macerate for 1 hour.

Whisk the egg whites until they form stiff peaks then fold them into the batter with the fruit mixture. Put tablespoons of the mixture into very hot fat and fry for a few seconds until golden brown. Drain on kitchen paper. Sprinkle liberally with castor (superfine) sugar and serve at once.

Serves 4-6

Cherry Pie

Clafoutis aux cerises

$1\frac{1}{4}$-$1\frac{1}{2}$ lb. black cherries
2 tablespoons ($2\frac{1}{2}$T)
  castor (superfine) sugar
1 tablespoon ($1\frac{1}{4}$T) brandy
8 oz. (2 cups) plain
  (all-purpose) flour
pinch of salt

3 eggs, separated
good $\frac{1}{2}$ pint (about $1\frac{1}{2}$ cups)
  milk and water mixed
2 oz. ($\frac{1}{4}$ cup) castor
  (superfine) sugar
$\frac{1}{2}$ oz. (2T) butter

Butter a 3 pint ($7\frac{1}{2}$ cup) ovenproof dish. Sprinkle the unstoned cherries with the 2 tablespoons ($2\frac{1}{2}$T) sugar and the brandy and leave for about 30 minutes.

Sieve the flour and salt into a bowl. Add the egg yolks and enough of the milk and water to make a pouring batter. Whisk the egg whites with the remaining sugar until they form stiff peaks, then fold them into the batter. Pour the batter into the prepared dish and spoon the cherry mixture over. Dot with butter.

Bake at 375°F, Gas Mark 5 for about 40 minutes until well risen, firm and golden brown. Serve with sugar and cream.

Serves 6

Peaches in Brandy

Pêches au cognac
To skin the peaches, drop them into boiling water for about one minute, then plunge them into cold water. The skins will then slip off easily.

4 oz. ($\frac{1}{2}$ cup) granulated sugar
$\frac{1}{2}$ pint ($1\frac{1}{4}$ cups) water
4 ripe peaches, skinned and
   halved

5 tablespoons ($6\frac{1}{4}$T) brandy

Dissolve the sugar with the water in a pan without boiling.
Remove the stones from the peaches and add the peach halves
to the pan. Simmer very gently until tender, then place the
drained peaches in a flameproof dish.
Boil the remaining syrup in the pan until reduced by two
thirds. Add brandy to the syrup and pour over the peaches.
Serves 4

Pears and Prunes in Red Wine

Poires et pruneaux bourguignonnes

$\frac{1}{2}$ pint ($1\frac{1}{4}$ cups) red wine
$\frac{1}{2}$ pint ($1\frac{1}{4}$ cups) water
4 oz. ($\frac{1}{2}$ cup)
   granulated sugar

1 inch piece of cinnamon stick
1 strip lemon peel
12 pears, peeled
8 oz. can of prunes, drained

Put the wine, water, sugar, cinnamon and lemon peel in a pan.
Remove the eye from the base of each pear but leave the stalks
on. Heat the wine mixture without boiling until the sugar has
dissolved.
Add the pears to the pan. Cover and simmer very slowly for
30 minutes or until tender. Remove the pears from the pan.
Put them in a serving dish with the prunes.
Boil the wine mixture for a few minutes until it is slightly
syrupy. Strain it over the fruit. Leave in a cold place until just
before serving. Serve with chilled cream.
Serves 6

Apricot Tart

Tarte aux abricots
This is equally delicious made with poached fresh apricots or peaches.

Rich shortcrust pastry flan case:

12 oz. (3 cups) plain (all-purpose) flour
$\frac{1}{2}$ teaspoon salt
1 tablespoon ($1\frac{1}{4}$T) icing (confectioners') sugar
4 oz. ($\frac{1}{2}$ cup) butter
3 oz. ($\frac{3}{8}$ cup) lard
about 9 teaspoons (3T) water

Confectioners' custard:

3 eggs
3 oz. ($\frac{3}{8}$ cup) castor (superfine) sugar
3 tablespoons flour
$\frac{3}{4}$ pint (scant 2 cups) milk
few drops vanilla essence

Fruit filling:

29 oz. can and
15 oz. can apricot halves

Arrowroot glaze:

3 teaspoons (1T) arrowroot
$\frac{1}{2}$ pint ($1\frac{1}{4}$ cups) fruit juice
2 tablespoons ($2\frac{1}{2}$T) apricot brandy

Make the pastry in the usual way. Use it to line an 11 inch shallow, fluted flan tin with a removable base. Line with greaseproof paper and baking beans, or with foil, and bake blind' at 400°F, Gas Mark 6 for 25 minutes. Remove the paper and baking beans or foil, and bake for a further 5 minutes to dry the base of the flan case. Remove from the oven and leave to cool.

Blend together the eggs, sugar and flour for the confectioners' custard. Boil the milk and pour onto the egg mixture. Stir well. Return to the pan, bring to the boil and simmer for 2-3 minutes until thick. Remove from the heat and stir frequently so that a skin does not form. Add the vanilla essence.

Spread the cold custard in the base of the flan case. Drain the fruit and arrange on top of the custard. Put the arrowroot in a pan, blend in the fruit juice and simmer until thick. Stir in the apricot brandy. Spoon or brush the glaze over the fruit and leave until set.

Serves 12

Profiteroles

Choux pastry:
2 oz. ($\frac{1}{4}$ cup) butter
$\frac{1}{4}$ pint ($\frac{1}{2}$ cup + 2T) milk and
  water, mixed
2$\frac{1}{2}$ oz. (good $\frac{1}{2}$ cup) plain
  (all-purpose) flour, sifted
2 eggs, beaten

Filling and icing:
$\frac{1}{2}$ pint (1$\frac{1}{4}$ cups) thick (heavy)
  cream, lightly whipped
8 oz. (1$\frac{1}{2}$ cups) icing
  (confectioners') sugar
1 tablespoon (1$\frac{1}{4}$T) cocoa
1 tablespoon (1$\frac{1}{4}$T) rum
1-2 tablespoons (1$\frac{1}{4}$-2$\frac{1}{2}$T)
  warm water

Put the butter, milk and water in a small pan and bring to the boil. Remove the pan from the heat, add the flour all at once and beat the mixture until it forms a ball. Gradually beat in the eggs to make a smooth, shiny paste.

Put the mixture in a large piping bag fitted with a $\frac{1}{2}$ inch plain nozzle. Pipe 20 blobs on to a greased baking tray. Bake at 425°F, Gas Mark 7 for 10 minutes, then reduce the oven temperature to 375°F, Gas Mark 5 for a further 15 to 20 minutes until golden brown. Split one side of each bun so the steam can escape. Cool on a wire rack.

Fill each bun with whipped cream. Sift the icing sugar and cocoa into a bowl. Stir in the rum and sufficient warm water to make a thick glacé icing. Spear each bun with a fork and dip the tops in icing. Pile up in a pyramid as each one is finished. Serve the same day.

Serves 6

PROFITEROLES *(Photograph: Cadbury Schweppes Food Advisory Service, Bournville, Birmingham, England)*

Scorched Oranges

Oranges brûlées
Serve very cold.

4 large oranges
2 tablespoons (2½T) Grand
   Marnier or Orange Curacao
two 5 oz. cartons (1¼ cups)
   soured cream

½ pint (1¼ cups) thick (heavy)
   cream, lightly whipped
2 oz. (¼ cup) Demerara (raw)
   sugar

Peel the oranges, removing all pith, and slice thinly. Place in
a shallow 2 pint (5 cup) ovenproof dish, sprinkle with the
liqueur. Blend together the soured cream and thick (heavy)
cream and spread over the oranges. Chill thoroughly in the
refrigerator.
Sprinkle the sugar on top Heat the grill (broiler) to maximum,
place the dish underneath. When the sugar has just melted
remove the dish from the heat.
Serves 4-6

Crêpes Suzette

*For entertaining, prepare both the pancakes and the sauce in advance and
assemble just before serving, heating the pancakes in the sauce.*

Batter:
4 oz. (1 cup) plain
   (all-purpose) flour
¼ teaspoon salt
2 eggs
scant ½ pint (1 cup) milk
1 tablespoon (1¼T) melted
   butter, or oil
1 tablespoon (1¼T) oil for
   frying

Sauce:
4 oz. (½ cup) castor
   (superfine) sugar
4 oz. (½ cup) butter
juice of 2 oranges
finely grated rind of 1 orange
1 tablespoon (1¼T) of either
   Curacao, Grand Marnier or
   other orange liqueur
3 tablespoons (3¾T) brandy

92

Sift the flour and salt into a large bowl. Add the egg, then gradually beat in the milk to make a smooth batter. Stir in the butter or oil.

Put the oil for frying in a 6 or 7 inch heavy based frying pan and heat slowly. When it is really hot pour off the excess oil and spoon about 2 tablespoons ($2\frac{1}{2}$T) of the batter into the pan. Tip the pan slightly from side to side so that the batter thinly covers the base of the pan. Cook the pancake for about 1 minute, then turn it over and cook for another minute. Put the pancake on a plate and cover with a clean tea towel.

Repeat with the remaining batter, stacking the pancakes on top of each other.

Put the sugar, butter, orange rind and juice into a pan. Heat gently until the sugar has dissolved, then simmer the sauce for about 5 to 10 minutes until syrupy.

Put a pancake in the pan, fold it in four, remove from the pan, place on a hot serving dish and keep it hot. Repeat with the remaining pancakes.

When they have all been coated add the liqueur and brandy to the pan, and replace the folded pancakes. Reheat the sauce gently then serve the pancakes.

Note   To flambé:
Add liqueur only to the pan before replacing the pancakes. Reheat gently. Warm the brandy, pour over the pancakes and set alight.
Serves 4

Index